JUNGLE ANIMAL ORIGAMI

Duy Nguyen

Sterling Publishing Co., Inc.
New York

Design by Judy Morgan
Edited by Claire Bazinet

Library of Congress Cataloging-in-Publication Data

Nguyen, Duy, 1960-
  Jungle animal origami / Duy Nguyen.
      p. cm.
  ISBN-10 1-4027-0777-0
  1. Origami. 2. Animals in art. 3. Jungle animals. I. Title.
TT870.N4863 2003
736'.982--dc21
                                        2003005848

10 9 8 7 6 5 4 3 2 1
  ISBN-13: 978-1-4027-7408-9
Published in paperback 2004 by Sterling Publishing Co., Inc.
387 Park Avenue South, New York, NY 10016
© 2003 by Duy Nguyen
Distributed in Canada by Sterling Publishing
℅ Canadian Manda Group, One Atlantic Avenue, Suite 105
Toronto, Ontario, Canada M6K 3E7
Distributed in Great Britain and Europe by Chris Lloyd at Orca Book
Services, Stanley House, Fleets Lane, Poole BH15 3AJ, England
Distributed in Australia by Capricorn Link (Australia) Pty. Ltd.
P.O. Box 704, Windsor, NSW 2756, Australia
Printed in China 07/09

Contents

Preface   4
Basic Instructions   4
Symbols & Lines   5

Basic Folds   6
kite fold ◆ valley fold ◆ mountain fold ◆ inside reverse fold ◆ outside reverse fold ◆ pleat fold ◆ pleat fold reverse ◆ squash fold I ◆ squash fold II ◆ inside crimp fold ◆ outside crimp fold

Base Folds 10
base fold I ◆ base fold II ◆ base fold III ◆ base fold IV

Creative Projects 16

Vulture	16	Water Buffalo	54
Hyena	22	Wildebeest	60
Hippopotamus	26	Orangutan	66
Giraffe	32	Zebra	70
Gorilla	36	Gazelle	76
Lion	42	Ostrich	82
Maned Lion	48	Elephant	88

Jungle Denizens 94   **Index 96**

Preface

Traditional "origami" suggests expressing oneself creatively through the art of folding paper, and folding paper exclusively—no cutting or pasting. Such origami can be pleasing in its simplicity and esthetically beautiful, but I prefer to allow myself the freedom to be fully creative. That's why, as in my previous books, I encourage you not to limit yourselves but to strive for a more natural look to your finished project. This comes into play even more here, with the addition of color to finish off your jungle animal creations. You can glue on extra layers or bits of colored paper, use marking pens or water colors, or even give your form a light coat of spray paint. A finished origami need not look exactly like those illustrations or forms you see here—or in other origami books. You can work wonders creatively. It's up to you to bring your original origami creations to life—with all its abundant variety.

Duy Nguyen

Basic Instructions

Paper: The best paper to use for traditional origami is very thin, keeps a crease well, and folds flat. You can use plain white paper, solid-color paper, or wrapping paper with a design only on one side. Be aware, though, that some kinds of paper stretch slightly, either in length or in width, while others tear easily. Packets of papers especially for use in origami (15 by 15 centimeters square, or a bit under 6 by 6 inches) are available in a variety of colors from craft and hobby shops.

Regular typing paper may be too heavy to allow for the many tight folds needed in creating more complex, traditional, origami figures, but it should be fine for the larger papercraft works, with fewer folds, given here. For beginners and those who have a problem getting their fingers to work tight folds, larger paper sizes are helpful. Slightly larger figures are easier to make than overly small ones.

Glue: Use a good, easy-flowing but not loose paper glue, but use it sparingly. Don't soak the paper as paints and coloring do not hold well to dried glue. This shouldn't be a problem, however, as most gluing is done between inner layers. A flat toothpick makes a good applicator.

Technique: Fold with care. Position the paper, especially at the corners, precisely, and see that edges line up before creasing a fold. Once you are sure of the fold, use a fingernail to make a clean, flat crease. Don't get discouraged with your first efforts. In time, what your mind can create, your fingers can fashion.

Finishing: If you used white or a solid-color paper for your origami, water paints or colored markers can add patterning or color that will make your creations, like the jungle animals in this book, "come alive"—after

Symbols & Lines

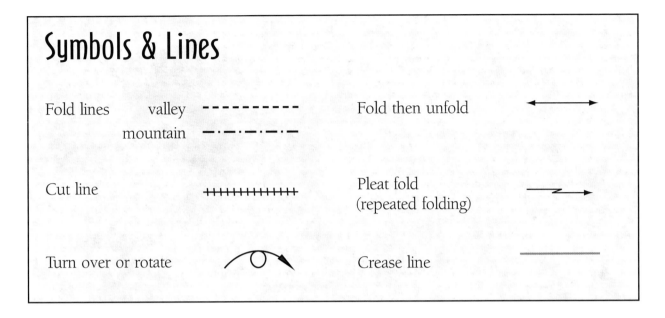

Fold lines   valley   - - - - - - - - -   Fold then unfold   ←——————→

              mountain   - · - · - · - ·

Cut line   ++++++++++++++++   Pleat fold (repeated folding)

Turn over or rotate   Crease line

all, a zebra without stripes is just a horse! So, once you have completed your form, look at it as the first step to a truly original creation. Have fun with it, but take your time and be careful. When working with paints, it's good to use plastic gloves. Hold figures, even upside down, so that excessive paint won't run to areas you don't want painted. If you use a spray paint, fix the form (or parts before assembly) onto a cut-off carton to hold it firmly. Lightly spray one side. Once dry, turn the form and do the other side. Most paper takes paint very well. Whatever materials you use, given thought and effort the results can be very satisfying—if not truly spectacular.

Squaring-Off Paper

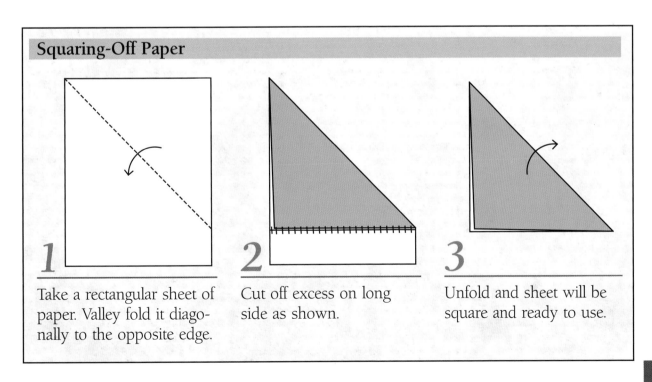

1 Take a rectangular sheet of paper. Valley fold it diagonally to the opposite edge.

2 Cut off excess on long side as shown.

3 Unfold and sheet will be square and ready to use.

Basic Folds

Kite Fold

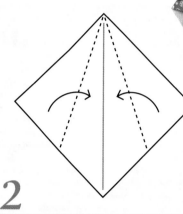

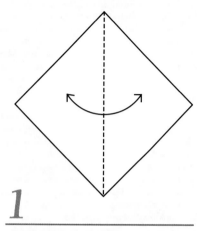

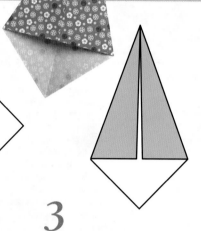

1

Fold and unfold a square diagonally, making a center crease.

2

Fold both sides in to the center crease.

3

This is a kite form.

Valley Fold - - - - - - - - - - - - - - - - -

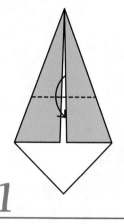

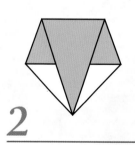

1

Here, using the kite, fold form toward you (forward), making a "valley."

2

This fold forward is a valley fold.

Mountain Fold — - — - — - — - — - —

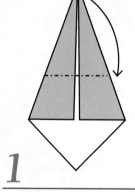

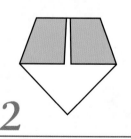

1

Here, using the kite, fold form away from you (backwards), making a "mountain."

2

This fold backwards is a mountain fold.

Basic Folds

6

Inside Reverse Fold

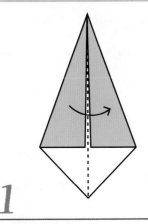

1
Starting here with a kite, valley fold kite closed.

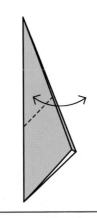

2
Valley fold as marked to crease, then unfold.

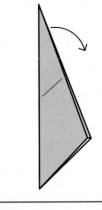

3
Pull tip in direction of arrow.

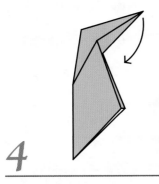

4
Appearance before completion.

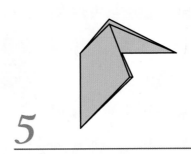

5
You've made an inside reverse fold.

Outside Reverse Fold

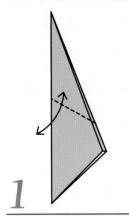

1
Using closed kite, valley fold, unfold.

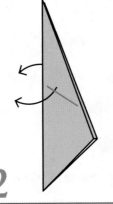

2
Fold inside out, as shown by arrows.

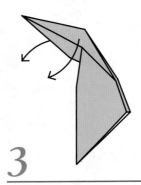

3
Appearance before completion.

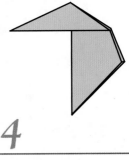

4
You've made an outside reverse fold.

Basic Folds

Pleat Fold

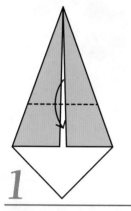

1
Here, using the kite, valley fold.

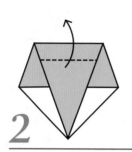

2
Valley fold back again.

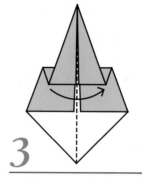

3
This is a pleat. Valley fold in half.

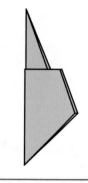

4
You've made a pleat fold.

Pleat Fold Reverse

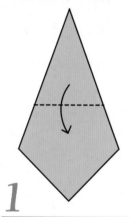

1
Here, using the kite form backwards, valley fold.

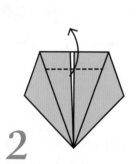

2
Valley fold back again for pleat.

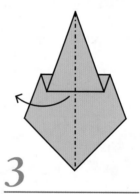

3
Mountain fold form in half.

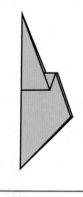

4
This is a pleat fold reverse.

Squash Fold I

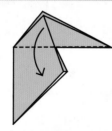

1
Using inside reverse, valley fold one side.

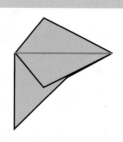

2
This is a squash fold I.

Squash Fold II

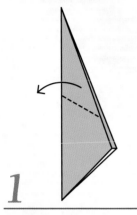

1

Using closed kite form, valley fold.

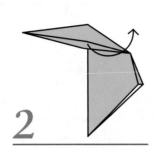

2

Open in direction of the arrow.

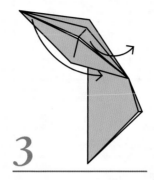

3

Appearance before completion.

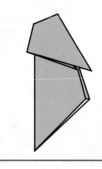

4

You've made a squash fold II.

Inside Crimp Fold

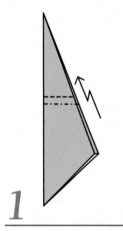

1

Here using closed kite form, pleat fold.

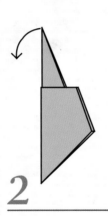

2

Pull tip in direction of the arrow.

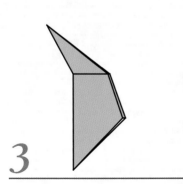

3

This is an inside crimp fold.

Outside Crimp Fold

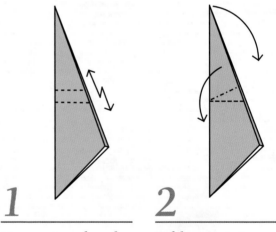

1

Here using closed kite form, pleat fold and unfold.

2

Fold mountain and valley as shown, both sides.

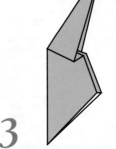

3

This is an outside crimp fold.

Base Folds

Base folds are basic forms that do not in themselves produce origami, but serve as a basis, or jumping-off point, for a number of creative origami figures, some quite complex. As when beginning other crafts, learning to fold these base folds is not the most exciting part of origami. They are, however, easy to do, and will help you with your technique. They also quickly become rote, so much so that you can do many using different-colored papers while you are watching television or your mind is elsewhere. With completed base folds handy, if you want to quickly work up a form or are suddenly inspired with an idea for an original, unique figure, you can select an appropriate base fold and swiftly bring a new creation to life.

Base Fold I

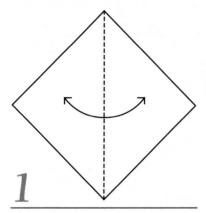

1

Fold and unfold in direction of arrow.

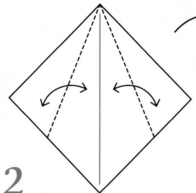

2

Fold both sides in to center crease, then unfold. Rotate.

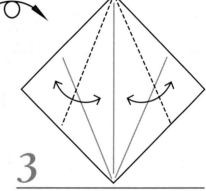

3

Fold both sides in to center crease, then unfold.

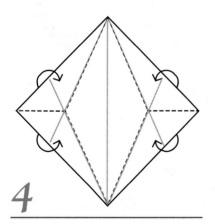

4

Pinch corners of square together and fold inward.

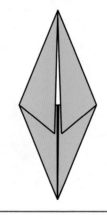

5

Completed Base Fold I.

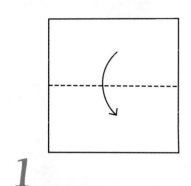

1

Valley fold.

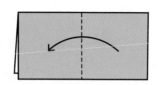

2

Valley fold.

3

Squash fold.

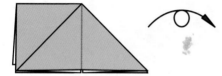

4

Turn over to other side.

5

Squash fold.

6

Completed Base Fold II.

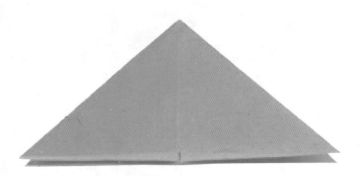

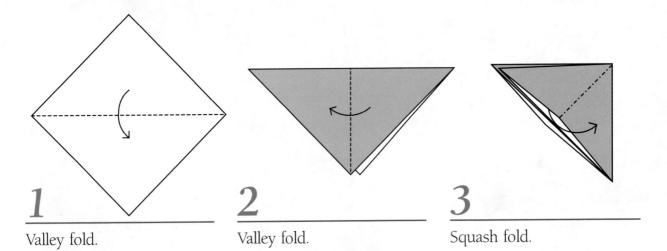

1 Valley fold.

2 Valley fold.

3 Squash fold.

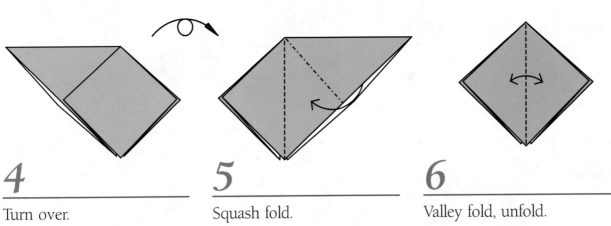

4 Turn over.

5 Squash fold.

6 Valley fold, unfold.

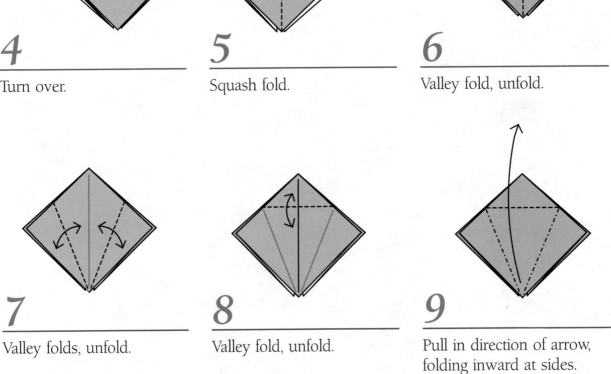

7 Valley folds, unfold.

8 Valley fold, unfold.

9 Pull in direction of arrow, folding inward at sides.

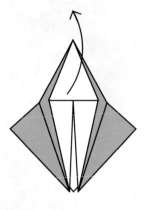

10

Appearance before
completion of fold.

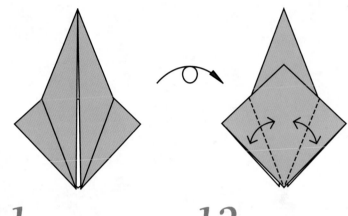

11

Fold completed. Turn over.

12

Valley folds, unfold.

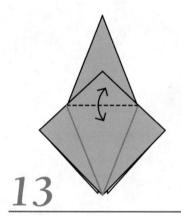

13

Valley fold, unfold.

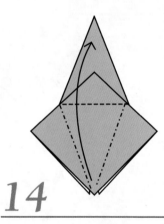

14

Repeat, again pulling in
direction of arrow.

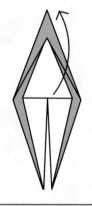

15

Appearance before
completion.

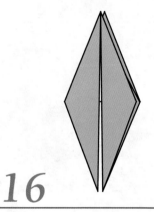

16

Completed Base Fold III.

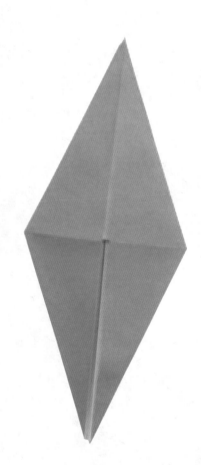

1

Valley fold rectangular size paper (length variable) in half as shown.

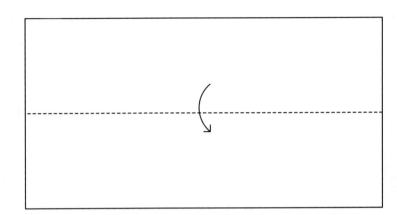

2

Valley fold in direction of arrow.

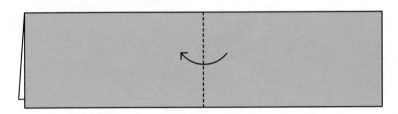

3

Make cut as shown.

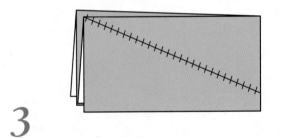

4

Unfold.

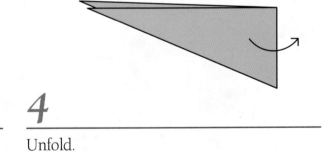

5

Unfold.

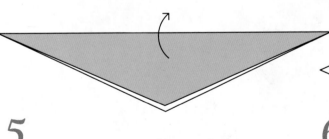

6

Valley fold in half.

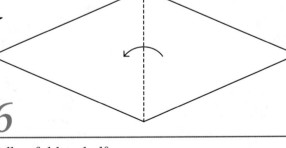

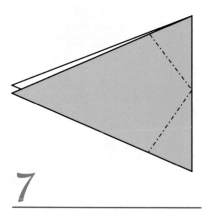

7

Inside reverse folds to inner center crease.

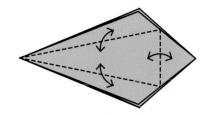

8

Valley fold and unfold to crease.

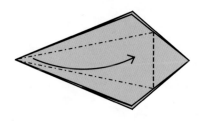

9

Pull in direction of arrow, and fold.

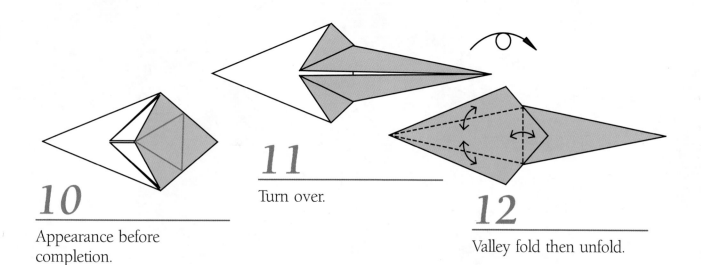

10

Appearance before completion.

11

Turn over.

12

Valley fold then unfold.

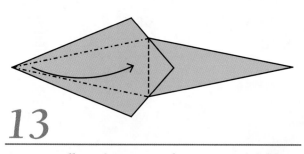

13

Again, pull in direction of arrow, and fold.

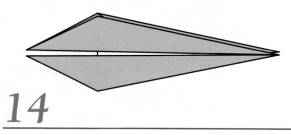

14

Completed Base Fold IV.

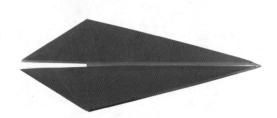

Vulture

Part 1

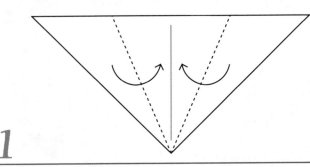

1

Start with square sheet of paper cut in half diagonally.
Valley fold to center along dashed line.

2

Unfold.

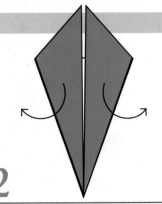

3

Valley folds.

4

Unfold.

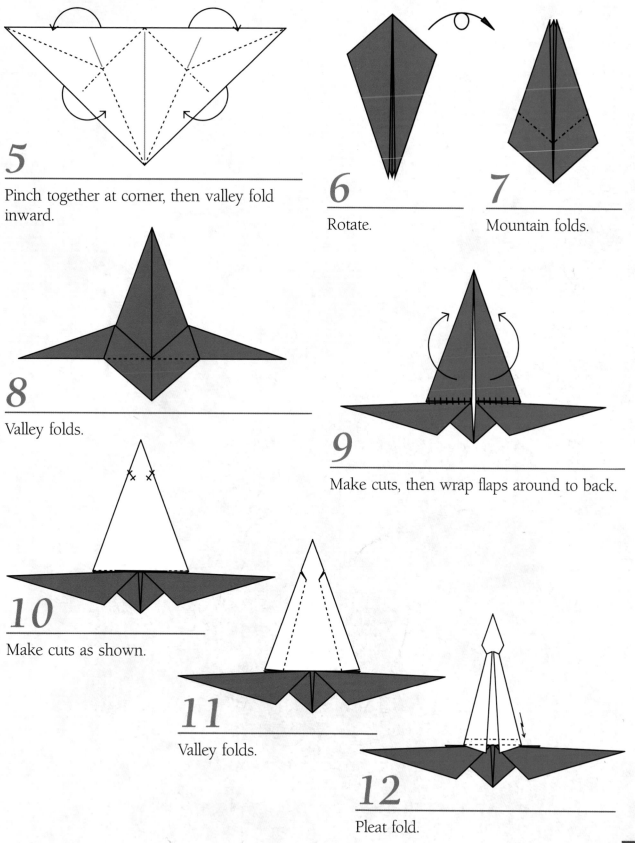

5
Pinch together at corner, then valley fold inward.

6
Rotate.

7
Mountain folds.

8
Valley folds.

9
Make cuts, then wrap flaps around to back.

10
Make cuts as shown.

11
Valley folds.

12
Pleat fold.

Vulture

17

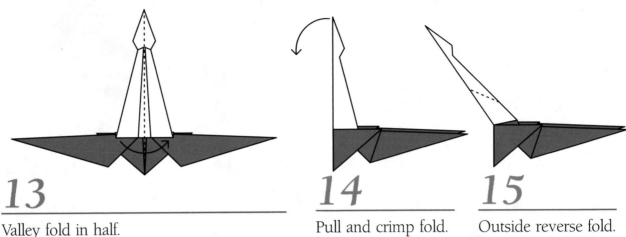

13

Valley fold in half.

14

Pull and crimp fold.

15

Outside reverse fold.

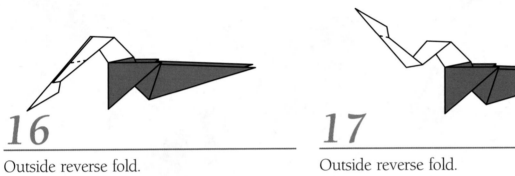

16

Outside reverse fold.

17

Outside reverse fold.

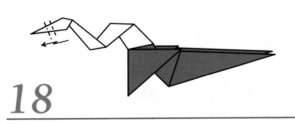

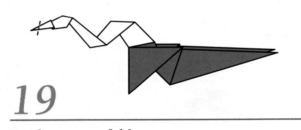

18

Pleat fold.

19

Inside reverse fold.

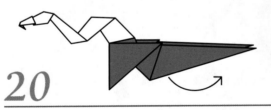

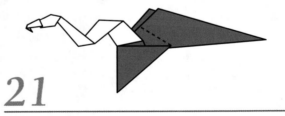

20

Mountain folds through inside, front and back.

21

Valley folds front and back.

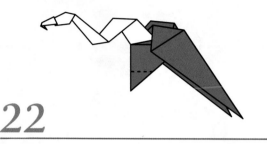

22

Inside reverse fold.

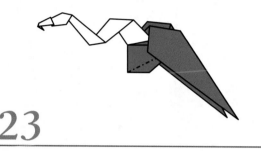

23

Mountain folds front and back.

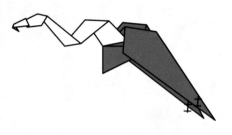

24

Make cuts as shown.

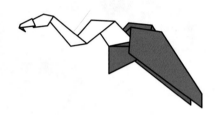

25

Complete part 1 (front) of vulture.

Part 2

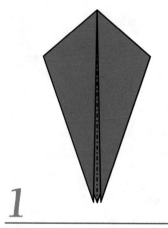

1

Start with Step 6 of Part 1, then mountain fold in half. and rotate.

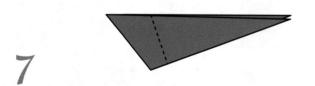

7

Valley folds to left, both sides.

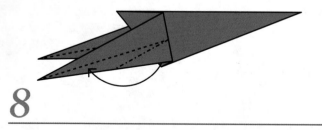

8

Valley and squash folds both sides.

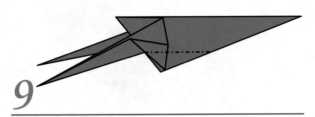

9

Mountain folds front and back.

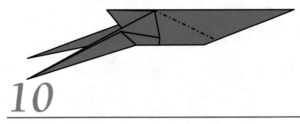

10

Inside reverse fold.

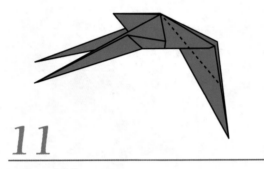

11

Valley folds.

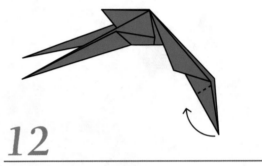

12

Outside reverse fold.

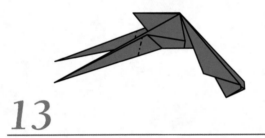

13

Mountain folds front and back.

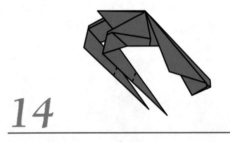

14

Outside reverse folds.

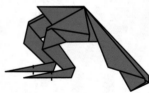

15

Outside reverse folds.

16

Valley folds to front and back, each foot.

17

Outside reverse fold, for back claws.

18

Complete part 2 (rear) of vulture.

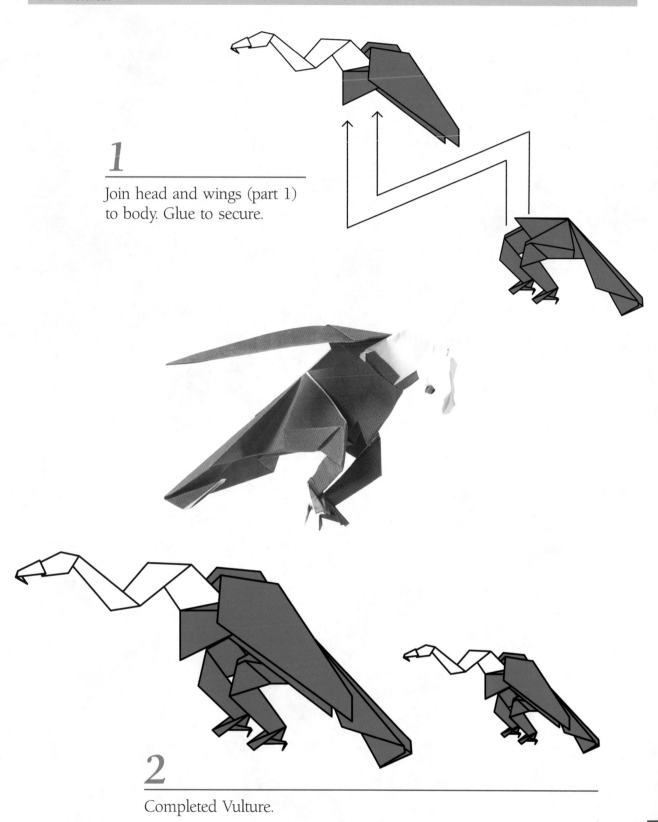

1

Join head and wings (part 1) to body. Glue to secure.

2

Completed Vulture.

Hyena

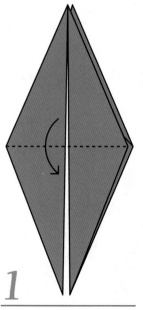
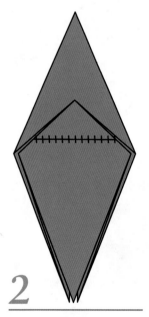
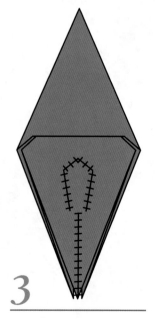
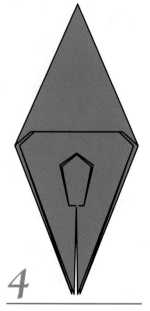

1
Start with Base Fold III. Valley fold.

2
Cut as shown.

3
Cut front layer only.

4
Valley fold.

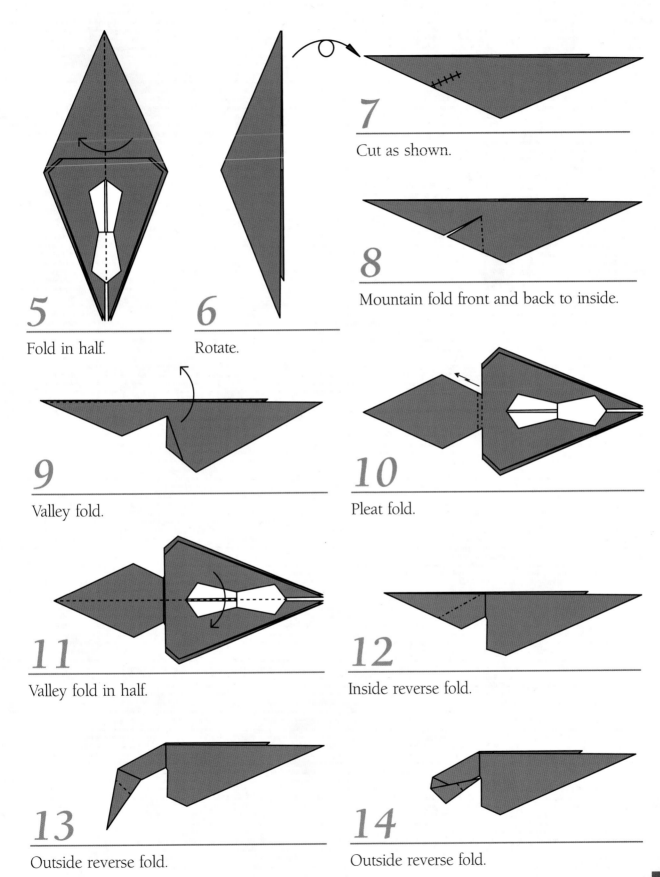

5

Fold in half.

6

Rotate.

7

Cut as shown.

8

Mountain fold front and back to inside.

9

Valley fold.

10

Pleat fold.

11

Valley fold in half.

12

Inside reverse fold.

13

Outside reverse fold.

14

Outside reverse fold.

Hyena

23

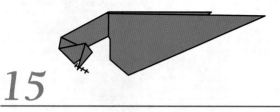

15

Cut tip slightly as shown.

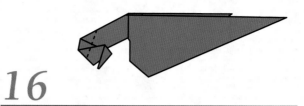

16

Valley fold both sides.

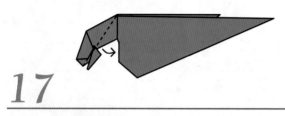

17

Valley fold.

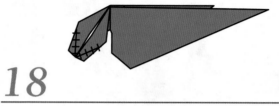

18

Cut front layers only as shown.

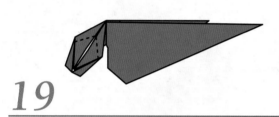

19

Valley folds.

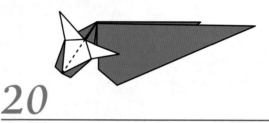

20

Valley fold.

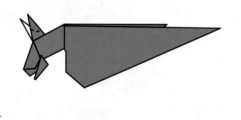

21

Valley fold both sides.

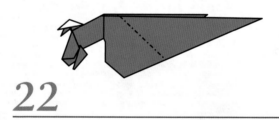

22

Inside reverse folds.

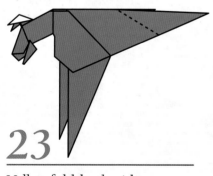

23

Valley fold both sides.

24

Valley folds.

25

Inside reverse folds.

26

Inside reverse folds, then rotate.

27

Mountain folds front and back.

28

Mountain folds again.

29

Outside reverse folds.

30

Pull and squash tail
into position.

31

Completed Hyena.

Hippopotamus

Part 1

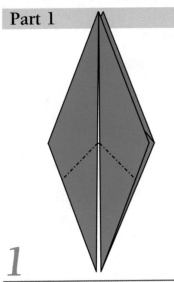

1

Start with Base Fold III.
Inside reverse folds.

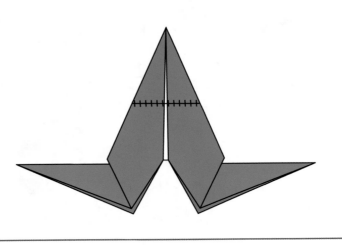

2

Cuts as shown.

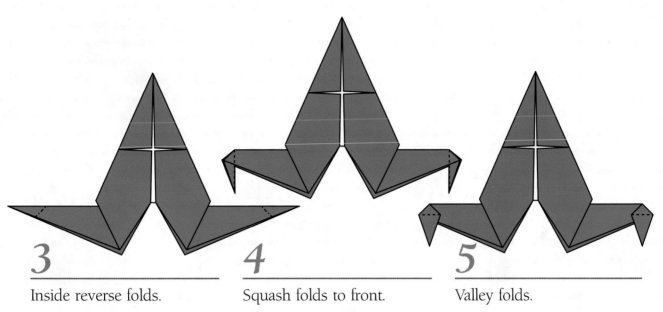

3

Inside reverse folds.

4

Squash folds to front.

5

Valley folds.

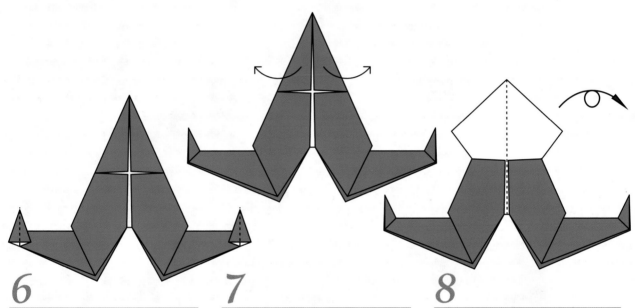

6

Valley fold top layers and crimp feet outward.

7

Open out as shown.

8

Valley in half, then rotate.

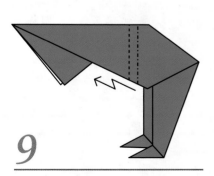

9

Pleat fold.

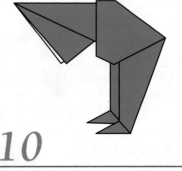

10

Unfold folds.

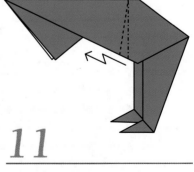

11

Pleat fold.

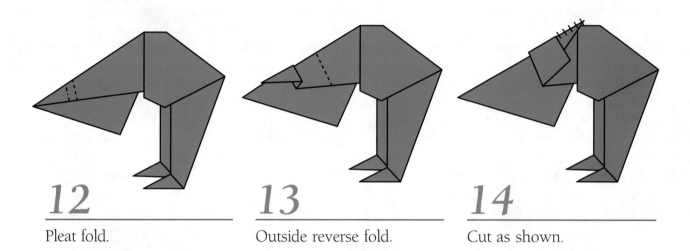

12
Pleat fold.

13
Outside reverse fold.

14
Cut as shown.

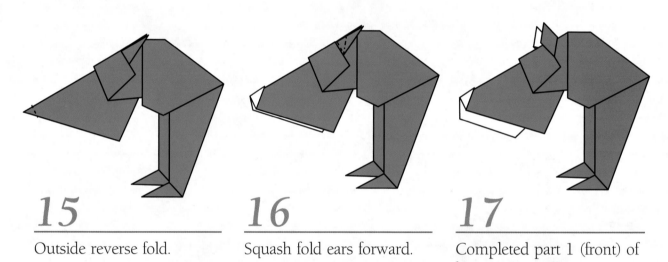

15
Outside reverse fold.

16
Squash fold ears forward.

17
Completed part 1 (front) of hippopotamus.

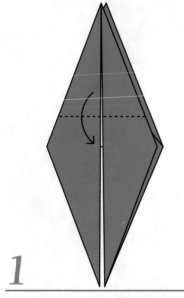

1

Start with Base Fold III.
Valley fold.

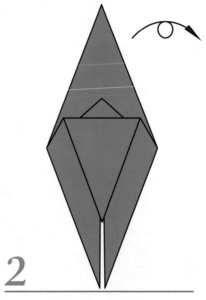

2

Turn over.

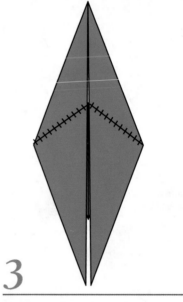

3

Cuts as shown.

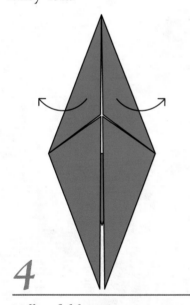

4

Valley folds.

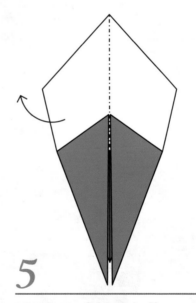

5

Mountain fold in half.

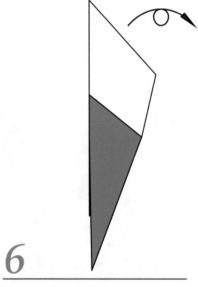

6

Rotate.

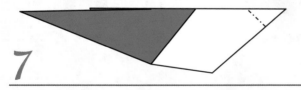

7

Inside reverse fold.

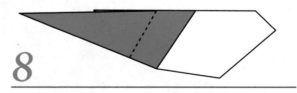

8

Valley folds both front and back.

Hippopotamus

29

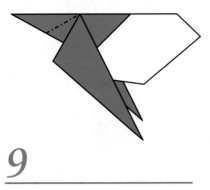

9

Inside reverse fold.

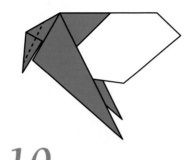

10

Valley fold both sides.

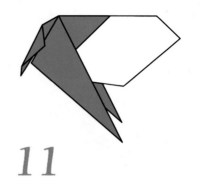

11

Secure tail behind layers.

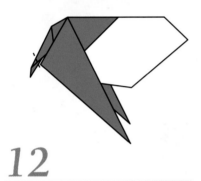

12

Cut as shown.

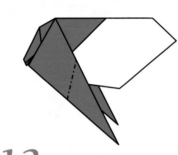

13

Inside reverse folds.

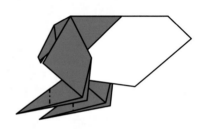

14

Inside reverse folds and rotate.

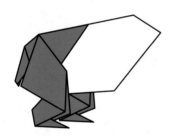

15

Completed part 2 (rear) of hippopotamus.

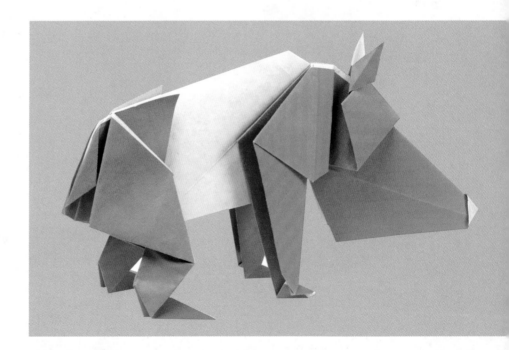

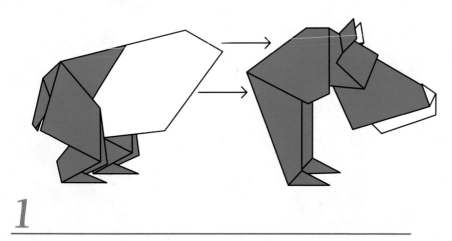

1

Join both parts together as shown and apply glue to hold.

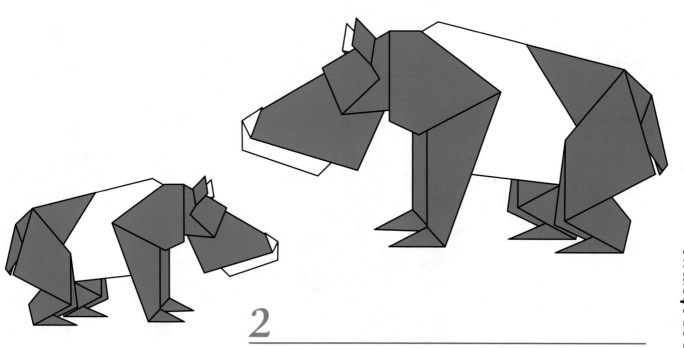

2

Completed Hippopotamus.

Giraffe

Part 1

1

Start with Base Fold IV, then valley fold.

2

Make cuts as shown. Rotate.

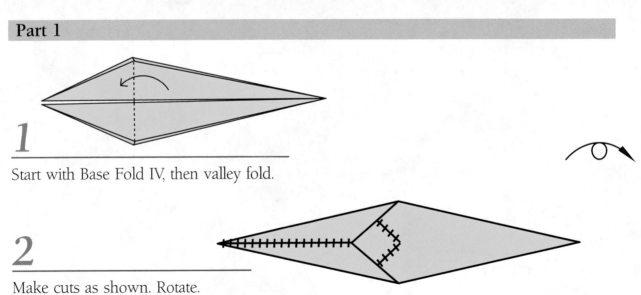

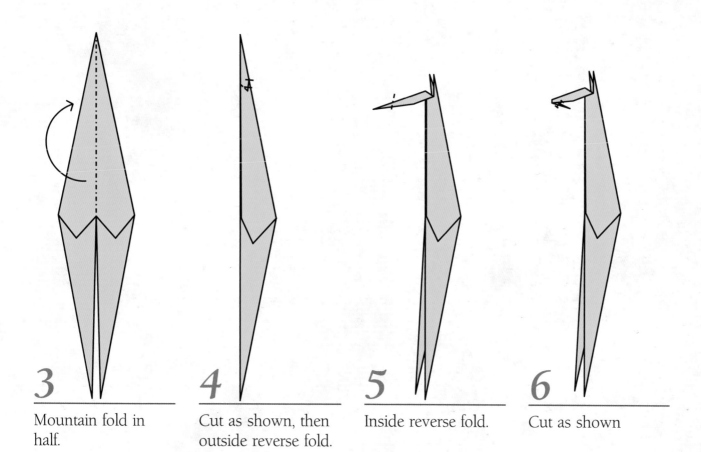

3
Mountain fold in half.

4
Cut as shown, then outside reverse fold.

5
Inside reverse fold.

6
Cut as shown

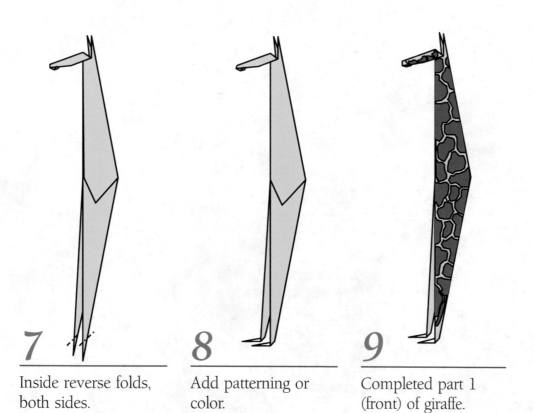

7
Inside reverse folds, both sides.

8
Add patterning or color.

9
Completed part 1 (front) of giraffe.

Giraffe

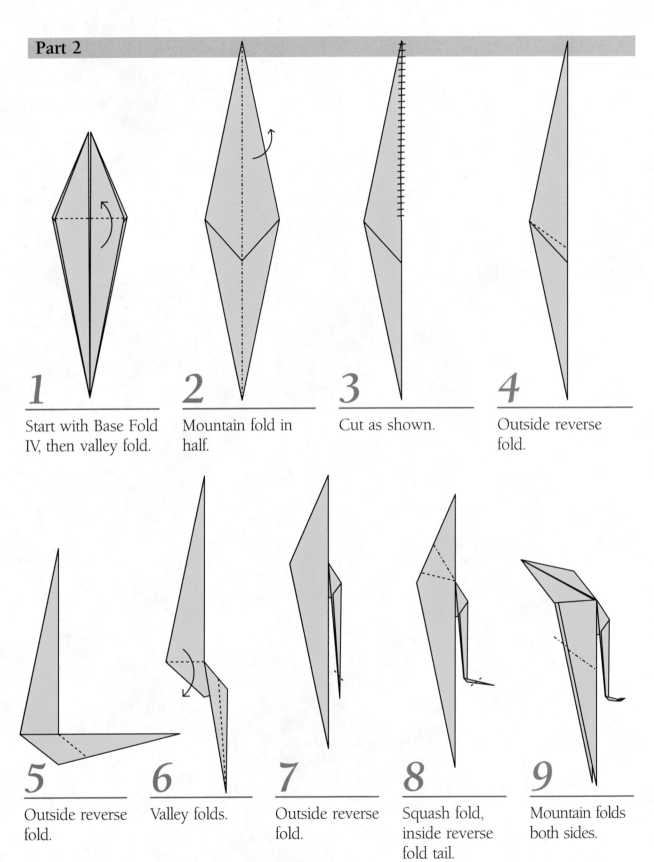

1
Start with Base Fold IV, then valley fold.

2
Mountain fold in half.

3
Cut as shown.

4
Outside reverse fold.

5
Outside reverse fold.

6
Valley folds.

7
Outside reverse fold.

8
Squash fold, inside reverse fold tail.

9
Mountain folds both sides.

Giraffe

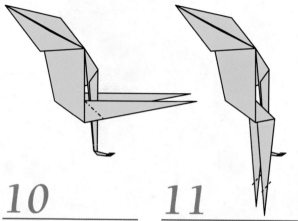

10
Repeat mountain folds.

11
Outside reverse folds.

12
Add patterning or color to completion.

13
Completed part 2 (rear) of giraffe.

To Attach

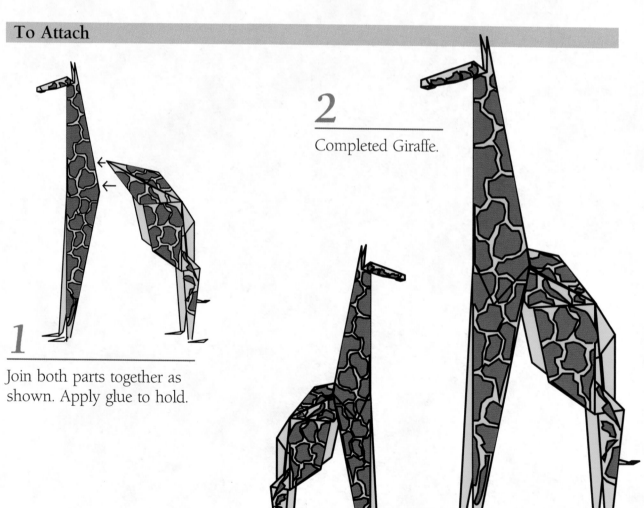

1
Join both parts together as shown. Apply glue to hold.

2
Completed Giraffe.

Gorilla

Part 1

1

Start with square sheet cut diagonally, then valley fold.

2

Inside reverse folds.

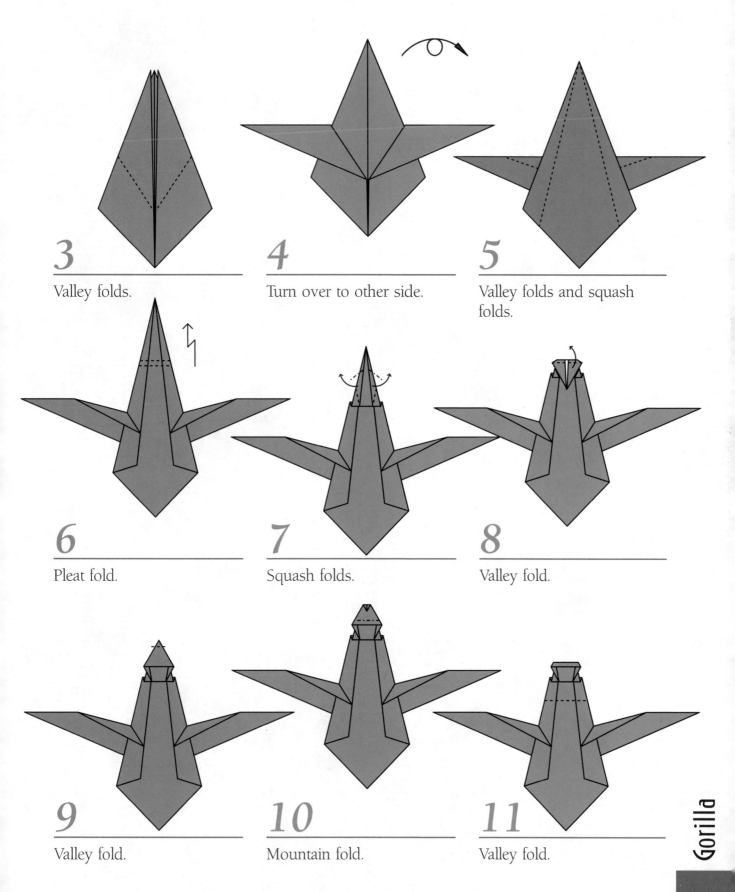

3

Valley folds.

4

Turn over to other side.

5

Valley folds and squash folds.

6

Pleat fold.

7

Squash folds.

8

Valley fold.

9

Valley fold.

10

Mountain fold.

11

Valley fold.

Gorilla

37

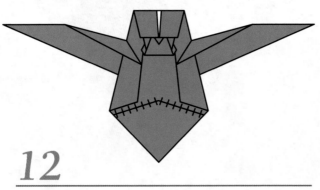

12

Cut as shown.

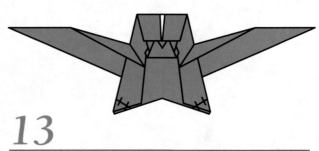

13

Cuts as shown.

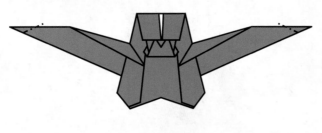

14

Inside reverse folds.

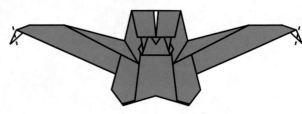

15

Outside reverse folds.

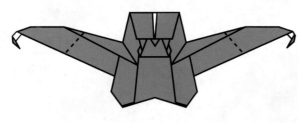

16

Valley folds.

17

Mountain fold in half.

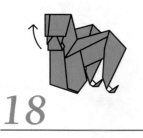

18

Pull and crimp head into position.

19

Pull and crimp open.

20

Unfold in direction of arrow.

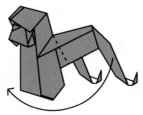

21

Valley fold both sides to extend arms.

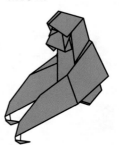

22

Completed part 1 (top) of gorilla.

Part 2

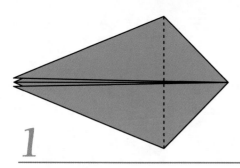

1

Start with step 3 of part 1, then valley fold.

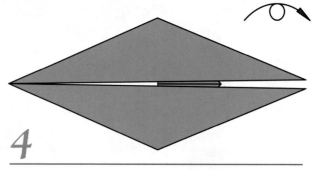

4

Turn over to other side.

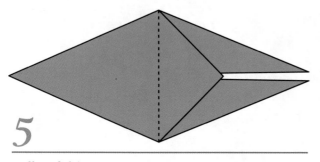

5

Valley fold.

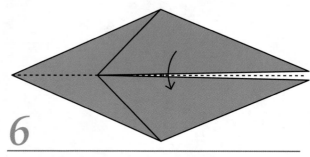

6

Valley fold in half.

Gorilla

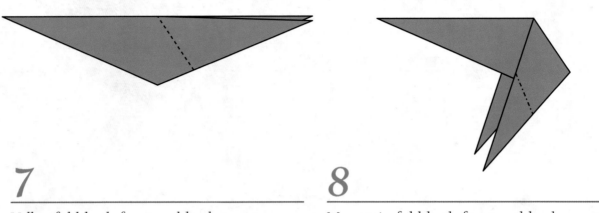

7

Valley fold both front and back.

8

Mountain fold both front and back.

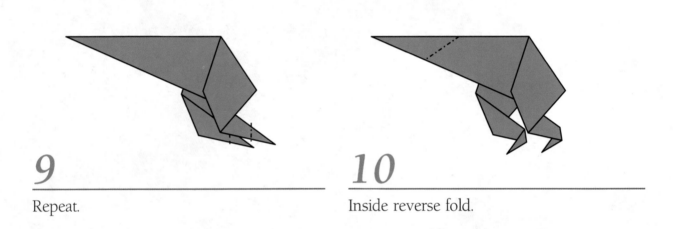

9

Repeat.

10

Inside reverse fold.

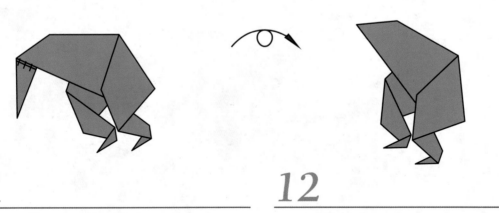

11

Cut as shown and rotate.

12

Completed part 2 (rear) of gorilla.

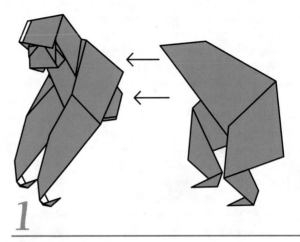

1

Join the two parts together as shown and apply glue to hold.

2

Completed Gorilla.

Lion

Part 1

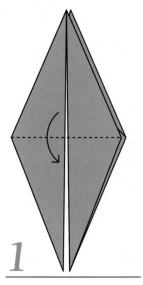

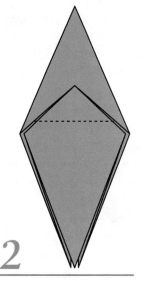

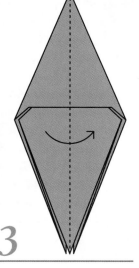

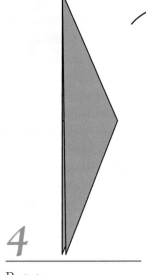

1
Start with Base Fold III. Valley fold.

2
Cut as shown.

3
Valley fold.

4
Rotate.

5

Inside reverse fold.

6

Outside reverse fold.

7

Repeat.

8

Cut as shown.

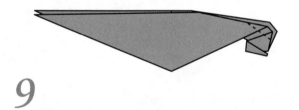

9

Valley folds front and back.

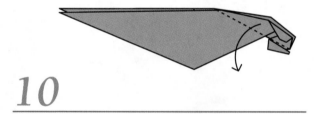

10

Valley fold.

11

Make cuts to front layers.

12

Valley fold cut parts.

Lion

43

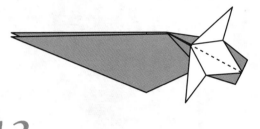

13

Valley fold back up into position.

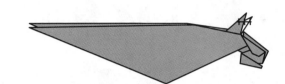

14

Trim ears, as shown.

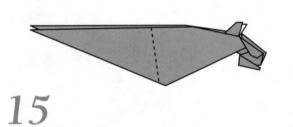

15

Valley folds front and back.

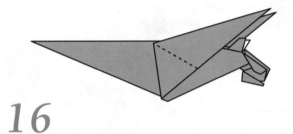

16

Valley fold both sides.

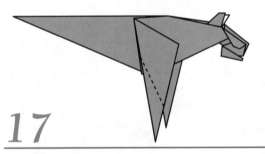

17

Mountain fold both sides.

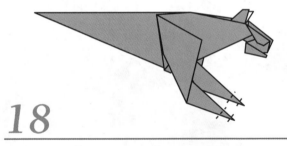

18

Valley and mountain fold each side.

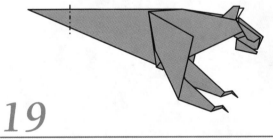

19

Inside reverse fold.

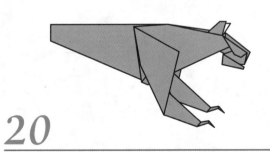

20

Completed part 1 (front) of lion.

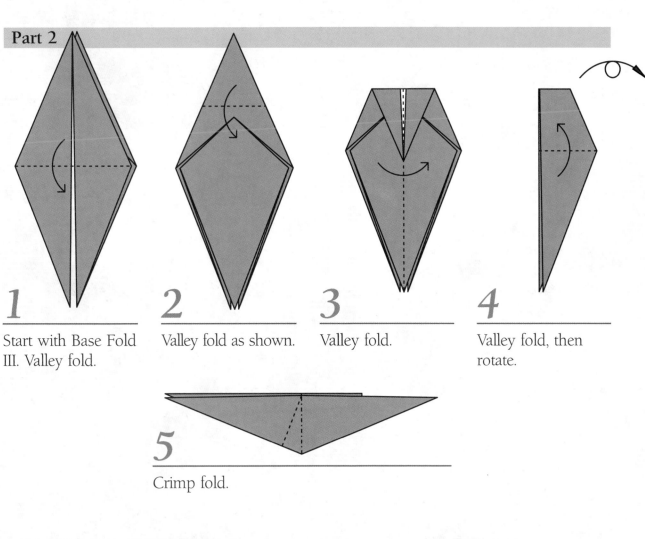

1
Start with Base Fold III. Valley fold.

2
Valley fold as shown.

3
Valley fold.

4
Valley fold, then rotate.

5
Crimp fold.

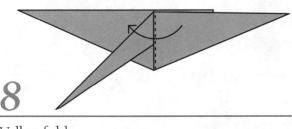

6
Cuts as shown.

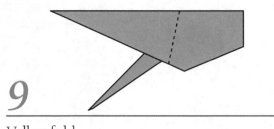

7
Mountain folds both front and back.

8
Valley fold.

9
Valley fold.

Lion

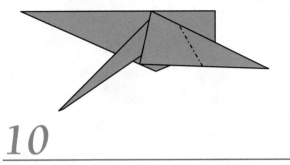

10

Inside reverse fold.

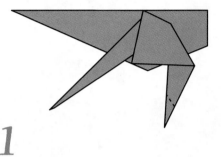

11

Inside reverse fold.

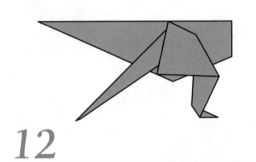

12

Turn over to other side.

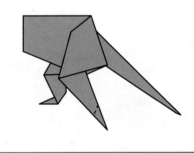

13

Valley fold.

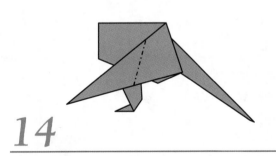

14

Inside reverse fold.

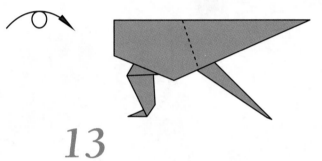

15

Repeat.

16

Valley fold.

17

Inside reverse fold.

18

Valley unfold tail tip.

19

Completed part 2 (rear) of lion.

To Attach

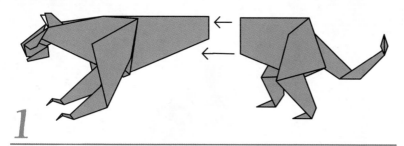

1

Join both parts together as shown and apply glue to hold.

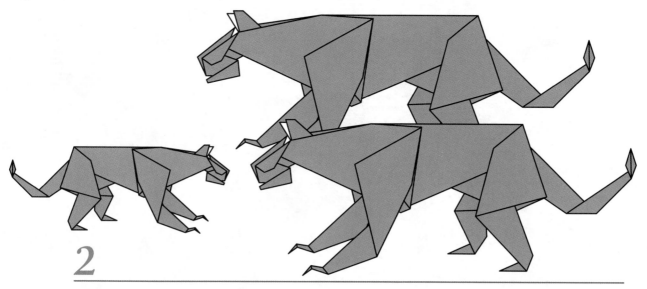

2

Completed Lion.

Maned Lion

Part 1

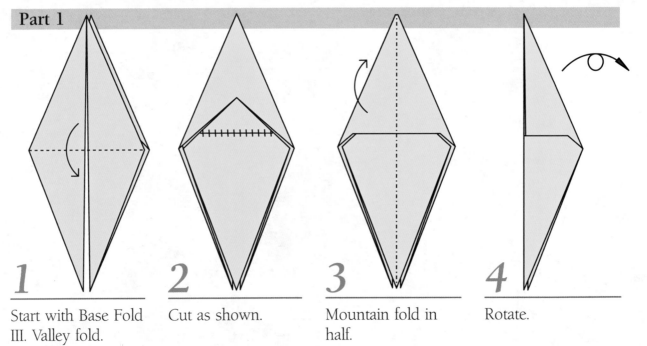

1
Start with Base Fold III. Valley fold.

2
Cut as shown.

3
Mountain fold in half.

4
Rotate.

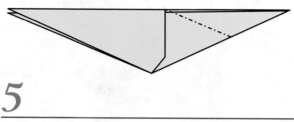

5

Inside reverse fold.

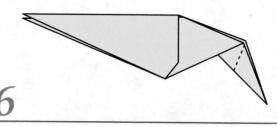

6

Outside reverse fold.

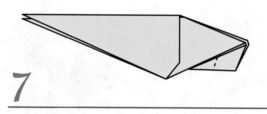

7

Repeat.

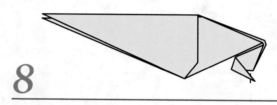

8

Repeat outside reverse fold.

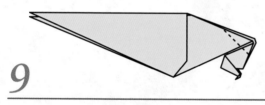

9

Valley fold front and back.

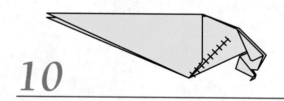

10

Cut as shown.

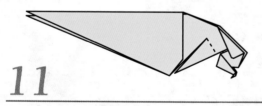

11

Valley fold both sides.

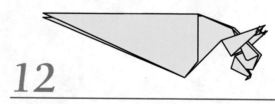

12

Cut as shown.

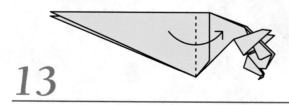

13

Outside reverse fold.

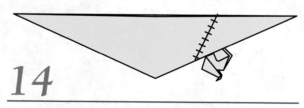

14

Cut front layers of both sides.

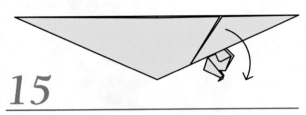

15

Valley unfold both front and back.

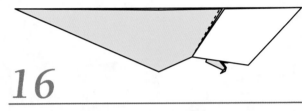

16

Outside reverse fold.

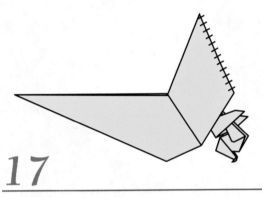

17

Cut as shown.

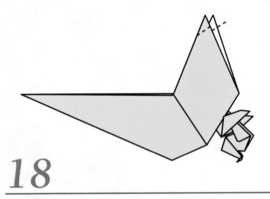

18

Valley fold both sides.

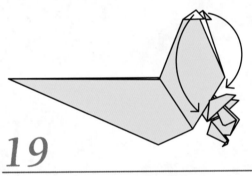

19

Pull folded tips down to sides as shown. Glue to hold mane in position.

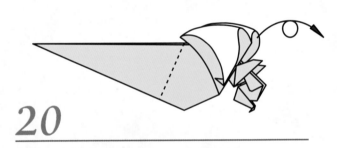

20

Valley fold both sides, and rotate.

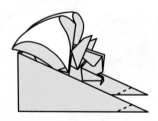

21

Outside reverse folds.

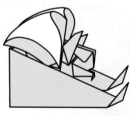

22

Repeat.

23

Make cuts to mane as shown.

24

Completed part 1 (front) of maned lion.

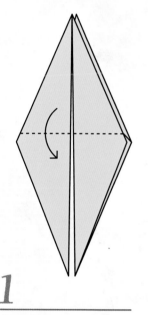

1

Start with Base Fold III. Valley fold.

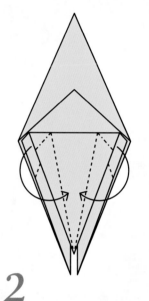

2

Squash folds.

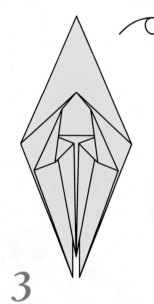

3

Turn over.

4

Cuts, and valley unfolds.

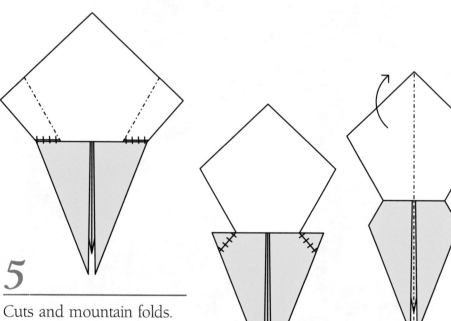

5

Cuts and mountain folds.

6

Cuts as shown.

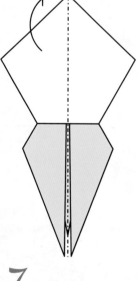

7

Mountain fold in half.

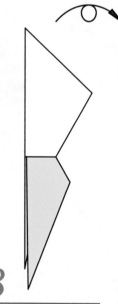

8

Rotate.

Maned Lion

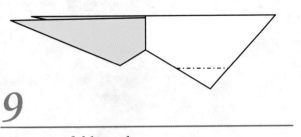

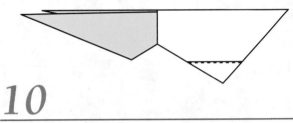

9

Mountain fold top layer.

10

Valley fold and apply glue to hold.

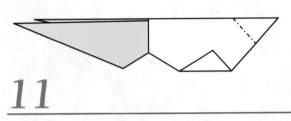

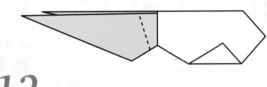

11

Inside reverse fold.

12

Valley fold both sides.

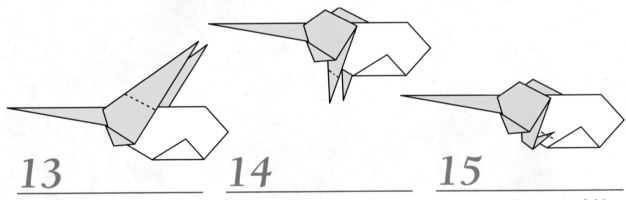

13

Inside reverse fold both sides.

14

Repeat.

15

Repeat inside reverse folds.

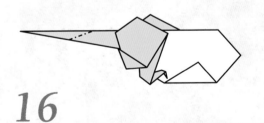

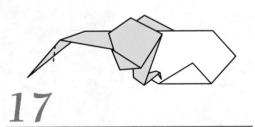

16

Mountain fold.

17

Valley fold.

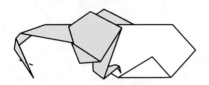

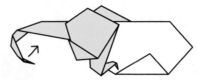

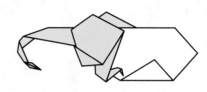

18

Inside reverse fold.

19

Valley fold.

20

Completed part 2 (rear) of maned lion.

To Attach

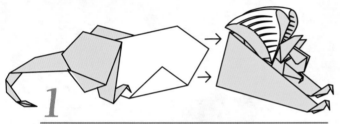

1

Join parts together and apply glue to hold. Add color and trim off unnecessary folds (on haunches) if you wish.

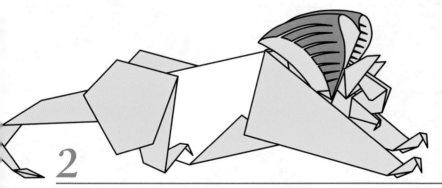

2

Completed Maned Lion.

Water Buffalo

Part 1

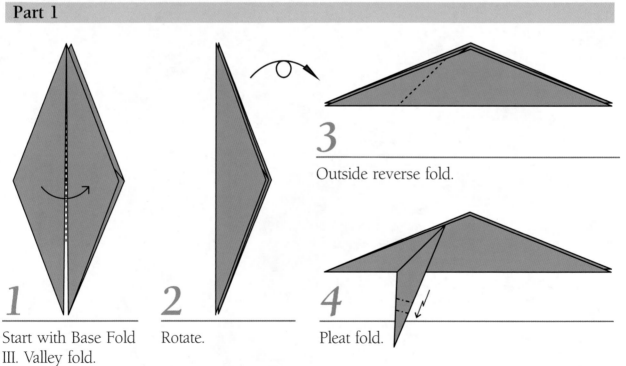

1

Start with Base Fold III. Valley fold.

2

Rotate.

3

Outside reverse fold.

4

Pleat fold.

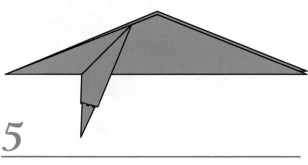

5

Outside reverse fold.

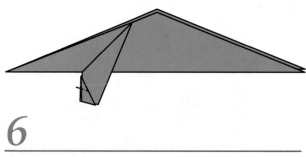

6

Inside reverse fold.

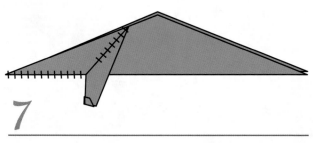

7

Make cuts as shown.

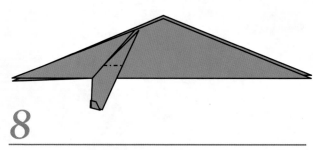

8

Mountain folds both sides.

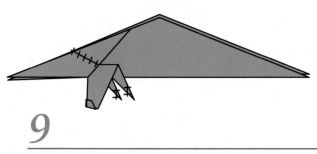

9

Make cuts as shown.

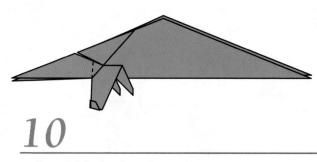

10

Valley folds both sides.

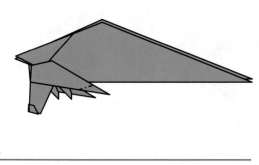

11

Mountain folds both sides.

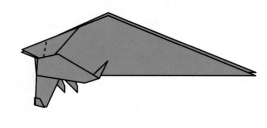

12

Valley folds both sides.

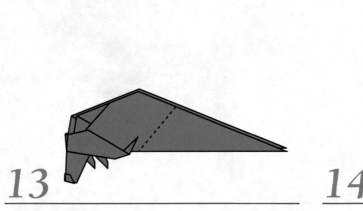

13

Inside reverse folds.

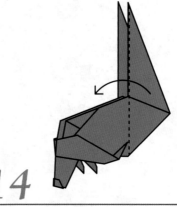

14

Valley folds both sides.

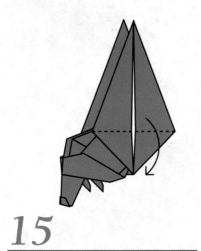

15

Valley folds both sides.

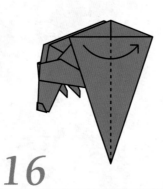

16

Repeat.

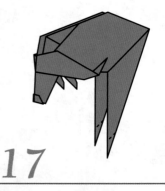

17

Outside reverse folds.

18

Valley fold then unfold.

19

Completed part 1 (front) of water buffalo.

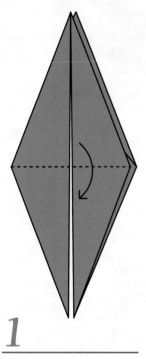

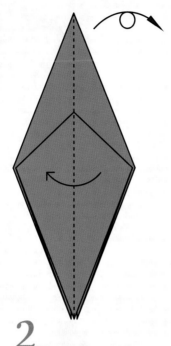

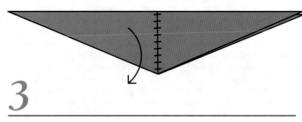

3

Make cuts to the first layer on both sides, then valley unfold.

1

Start with Base Fold III. Valley fold.

2

Valley fold and rotate.

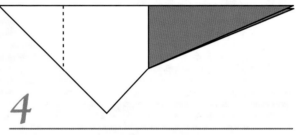

4

Outside reverse folds.

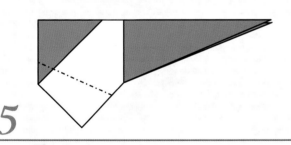

5

Mountain fold both sides.

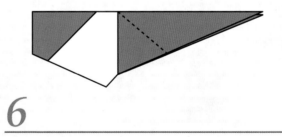

6

Valley folds.

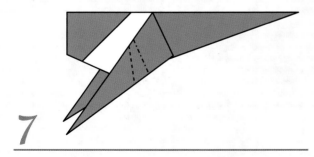

7

Crimp fold legs into place, both sides.

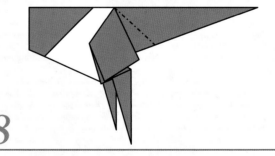

8

Inside reverse fold.

Water Buffalo

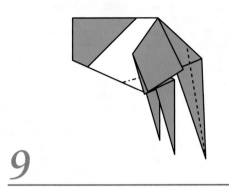

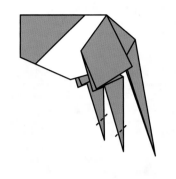

9

Valley folds to tail, mountain body inward.

10

Outside reverse folds.

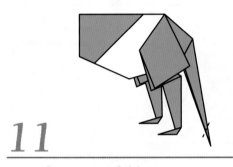

11

Outside reverse fold.

12

Completed part 2 (rear) of water buffalo.

To Attach

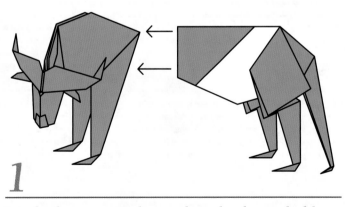

1

Join both parts together and apply glue to hold.

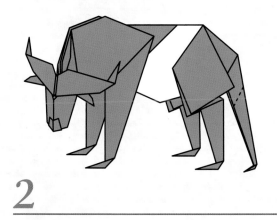

2

Valley fold, then…

3

…mountain fold, to give tail "life."

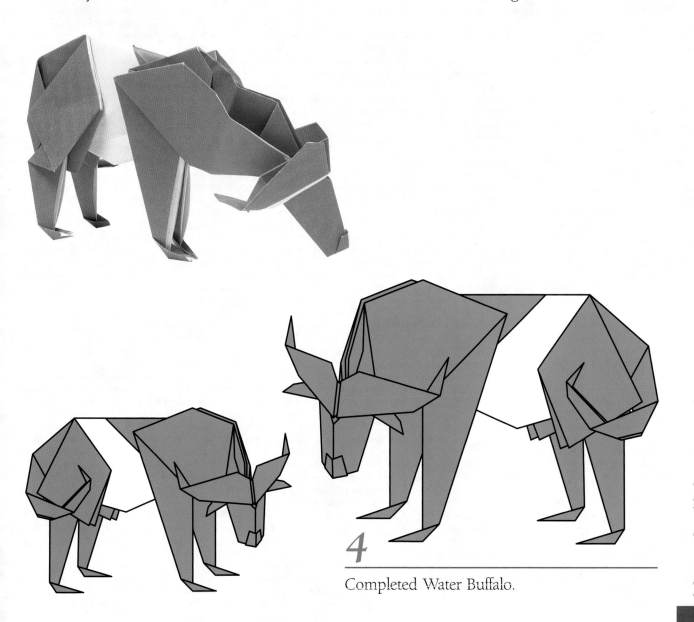

4

Completed Water Buffalo.

Wildebeest

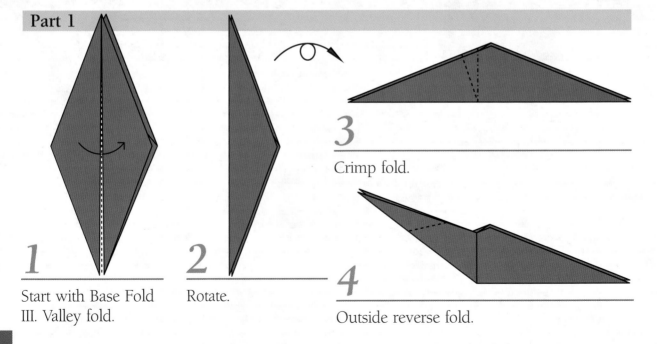

Part 1

1
Start with Base Fold III. Valley fold.

2
Rotate.

3
Crimp fold.

4
Outside reverse fold.

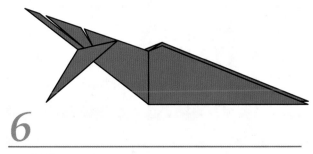

5

Cuts as shown.

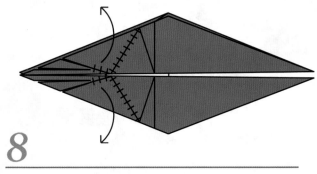

6

Unfold to return to step 3 position.

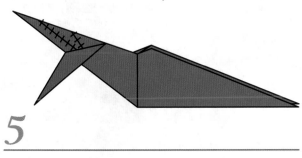

7

Valley unfold.

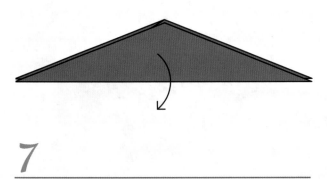

8

Cut front layers and valley fold cut flaps.

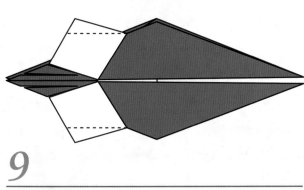

9

Valley folds.

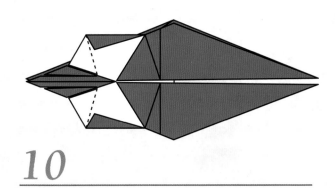

10

Valley folds.

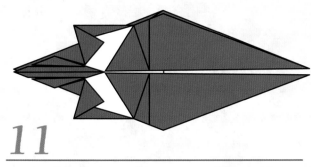

11

Repeat steps 3 and 4.

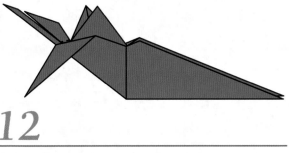

12

Valley fold both sides.

Orangutan

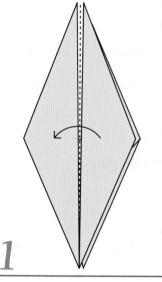

1

Start with Base Fold III.
Valley fold both sides.

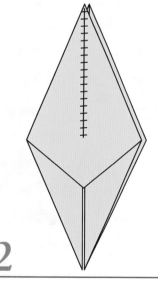

2

Cut as shown.

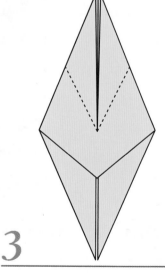

3

Valley folds.

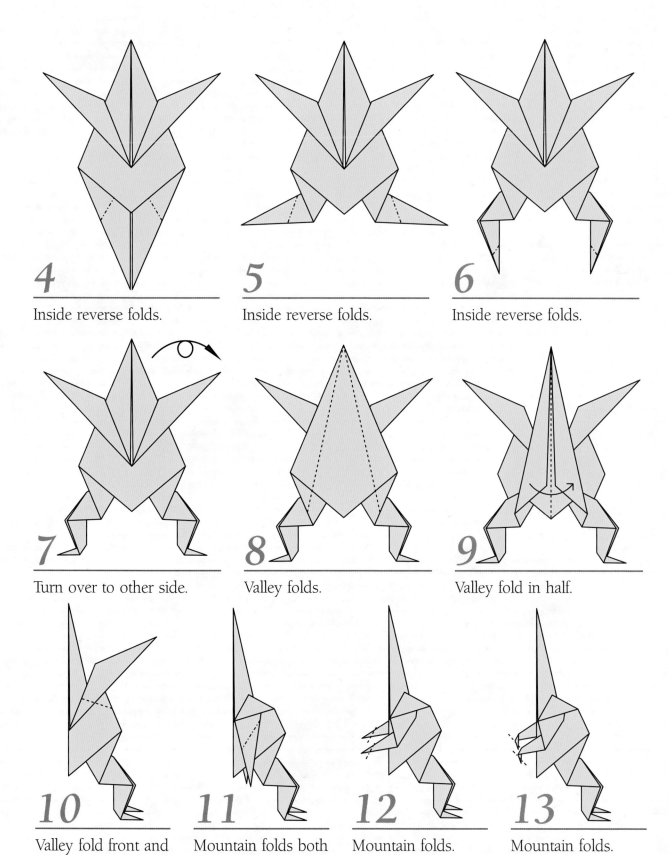

4

Inside reverse folds.

5

Inside reverse folds.

6

Inside reverse folds.

7

Turn over to other side.

8

Valley folds.

9

Valley fold in half.

10

Valley fold front and back

11

Mountain folds both sides.

12

Mountain folds.

13

Mountain folds.

Orangutan

67

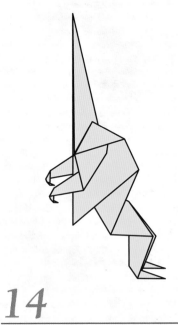

14

Mountain unfold.

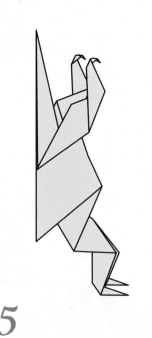

15

Mountain unfold, to open.

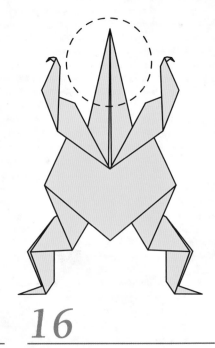

16

See close-ups for details.

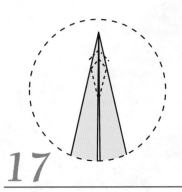

17

Squash sides outward, and pleat top flap.

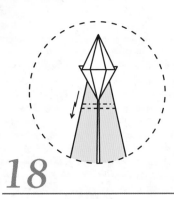

18

Pleat fold.

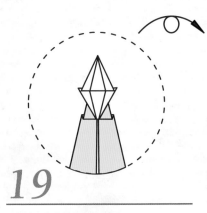

19

Turn over.

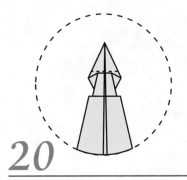

20

Valley fold.

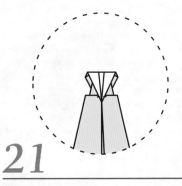

21

Valley fold.

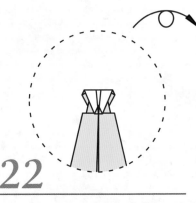

22

Turn over. Return to full view.

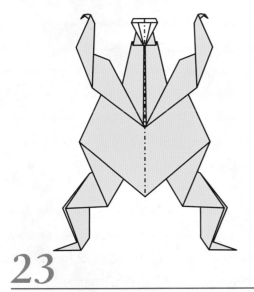

23

Mountain fold in half.

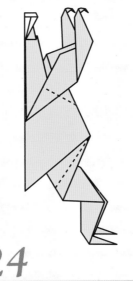

24

Valley folds both sides.

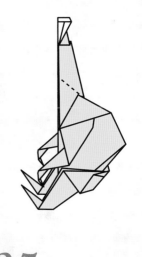

25

Outside reverse fold.

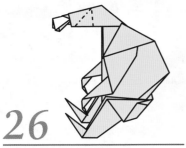

26

Pleat and crimp fold.

27

Pull and crimp into position.

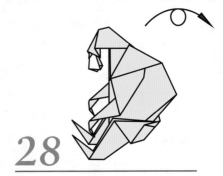

28

Open out body and rotate to completion.

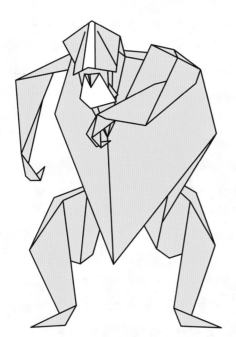

29

Completed Orangutan.

Zebra

Part 1

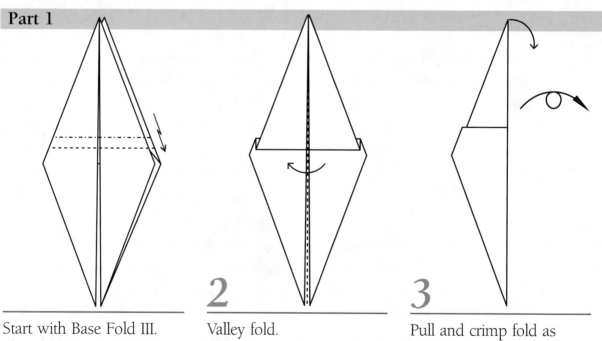

Start with Base Fold III.
Pleat fold.

2

Valley fold.

3

Pull and crimp fold as
shown, then rotate.

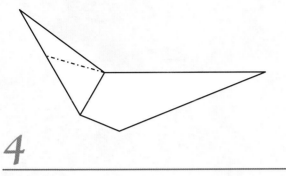

4
_____

Inside reverse fold.

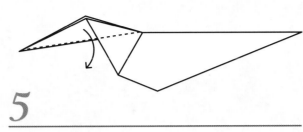

5
_____

Valley fold.

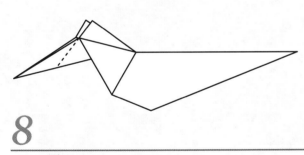

6
_____

Make cuts then valley unfold.

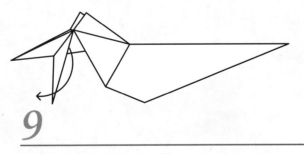

7
_____

Valley fold.

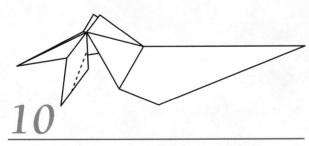

8
_____

Outside reverse fold.

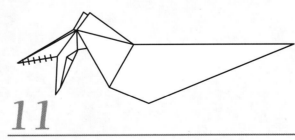

9
_____

Pull some paper out from inside.

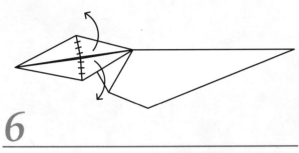

10
_____

Valley folds both front and back.

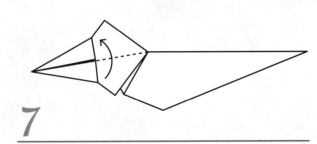

11
_____

Make cut as shown.

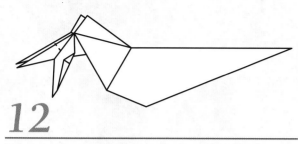

12

Valley fold both front and back.

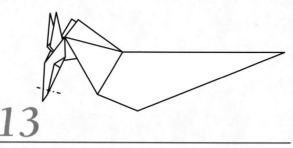

13

Inside reverse fold.

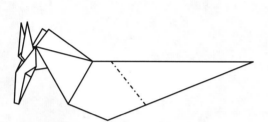

14

Inside reverse fold.

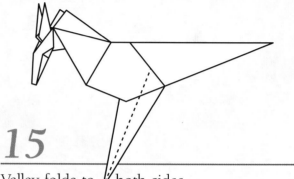

15

Valley folds to both sides.

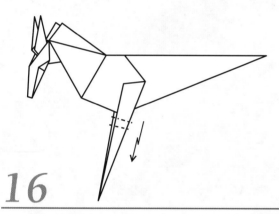

16

Pleat and crimp fold.

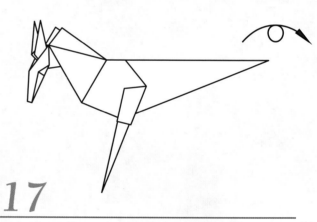

17

Turn over to other side.

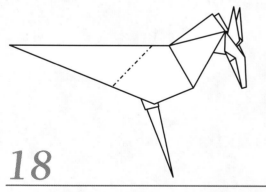

18

Inside reverse fold.

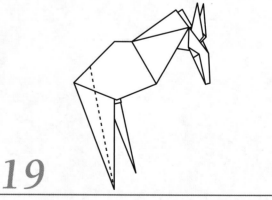

19

Valley folds to both sides.

20

Pleat and crimp.

21

Make cuts into mane, and add pattern.

22

Completed part 1 (front) of zebra.

Part 2

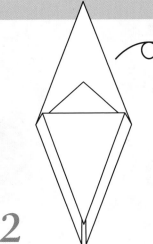

1

Start with Base Fold III. Valley fold.

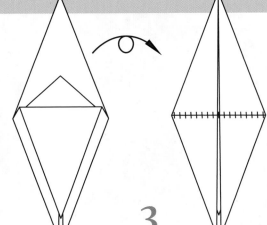

2

Turn over.

3

Cuts as shown.

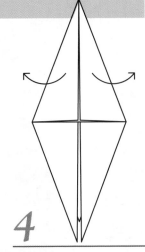

4

Valley folds.

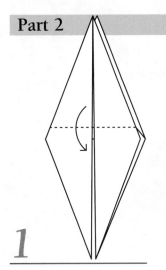

5

Cuts and mountain folds.

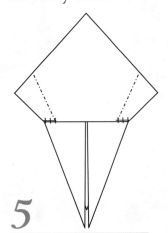

6

Turn over to other side.

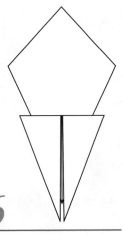

7

Valley fold.

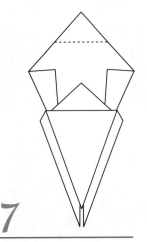

8

Valley fold in half and rotate.

Zebra

73

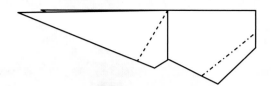

9

Valley fold, and mountain folds both sides.

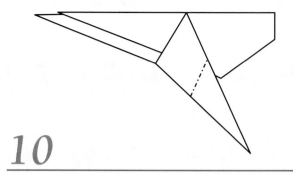

10

Inside reverse fold.

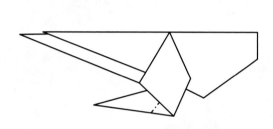

11

Inside reverse fold.

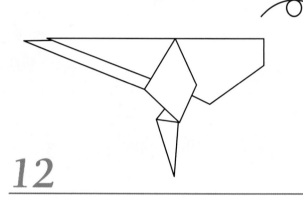

12

Turn over to other side.

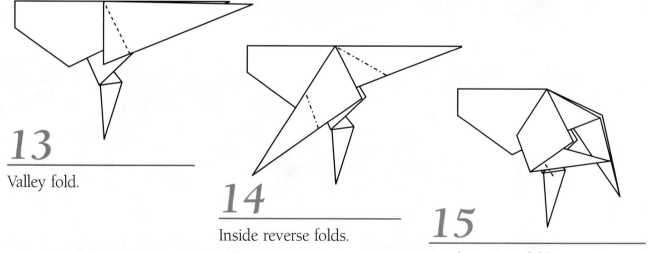

13

Valley fold.

14

Inside reverse folds.

15

Inside reverse fold.

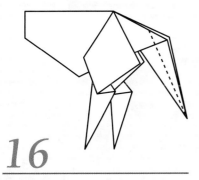

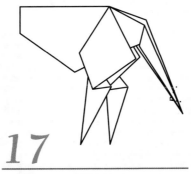

16

Valley fold to both sides.

17

Squash fold tail, and add pattern.

18

Completed part 2 (rear) of zebra.

To Attach

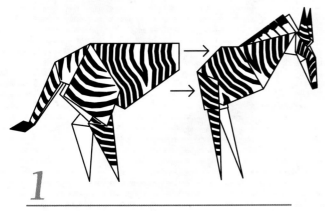

1

Join both parts together and apply glue to hold.

2

Completed Zebra.

Zebra

Gazelle

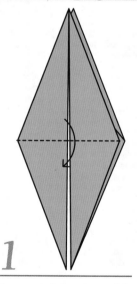

1

Start with Base Fold
III. Valley fold.

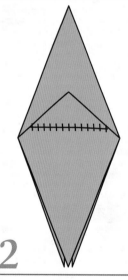

2

Cut as shown.

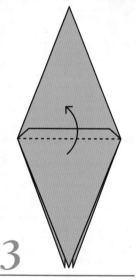

3

Valley fold.

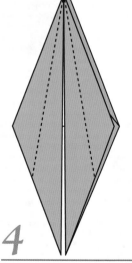

4

Valley folds both
sides.

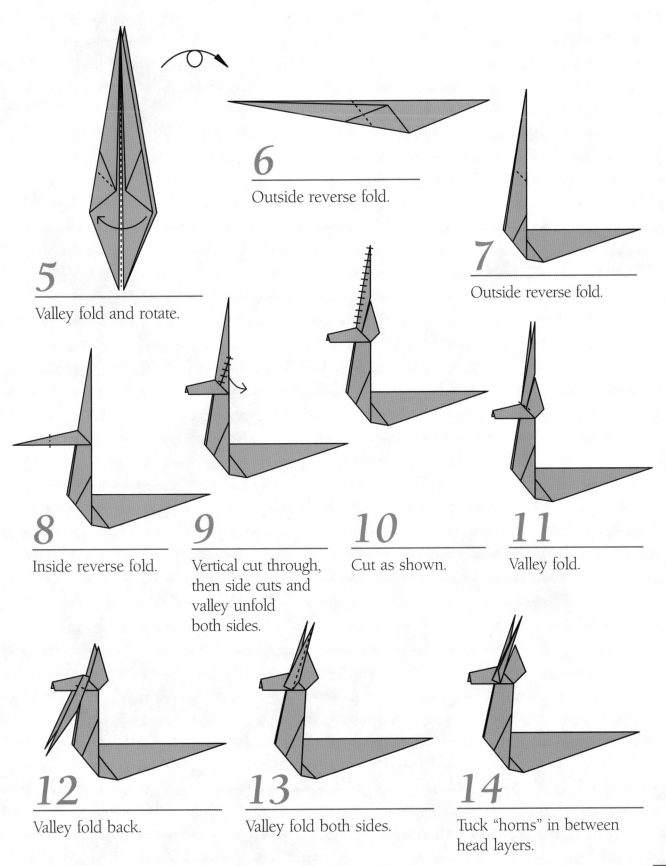

5

Valley fold and rotate.

6

Outside reverse fold.

7

Outside reverse fold.

8

Inside reverse fold.

9

Vertical cut through, then side cuts and valley unfold both sides.

10

Cut as shown.

11

Valley fold.

12

Valley fold back.

13

Valley fold both sides.

14

Tuck "horns" in between head layers.

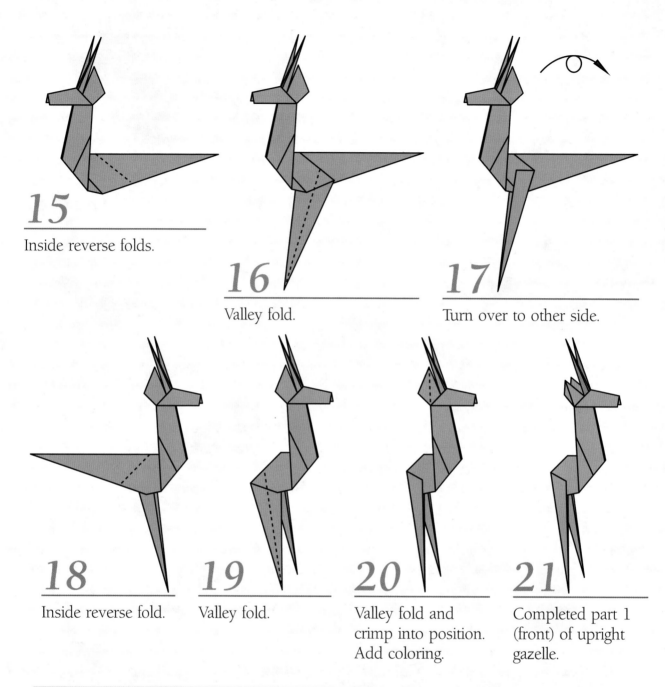

15
Inside reverse folds.

16
Valley fold.

17
Turn over to other side.

18
Inside reverse fold.

19
Valley fold.

20
Valley fold and crimp into position. Add coloring.

21
Completed part 1 (front) of upright gazelle.

Part 1 (grazing)

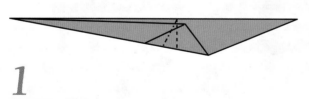

1
Start at step 6 of upright gazelle (page 76) and crimp fold.

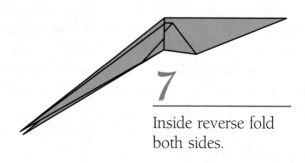

7
Inside reverse fold both sides.

Gazelle

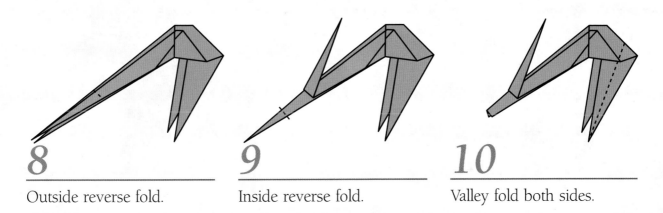

8
Outside reverse fold.

9
Inside reverse fold.

10
Valley fold both sides.

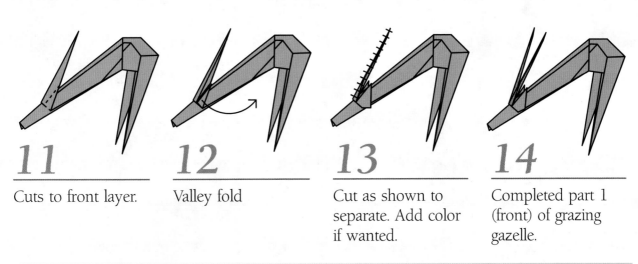

11
Cuts to front layer.

12
Valley fold

13
Cut as shown to separate. Add color if wanted.

14
Completed part 1 (front) of grazing gazelle.

Part 2

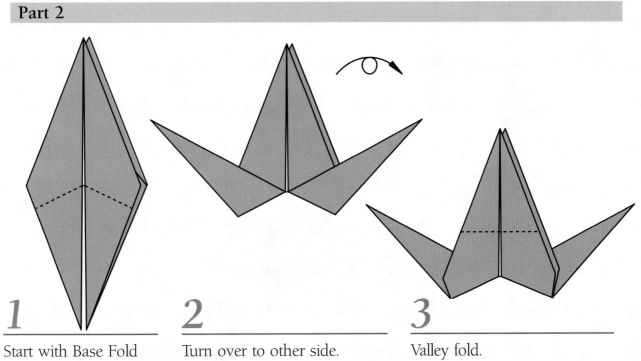

1
Start with Base Fold III. Valley folds.

2
Turn over to other side.

3
Valley fold.

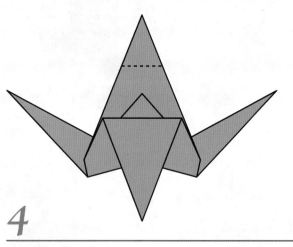

4

Valley fold.

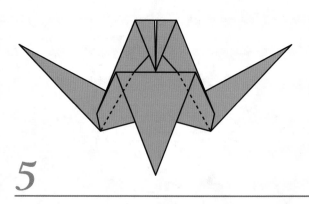

5

Valley folds.

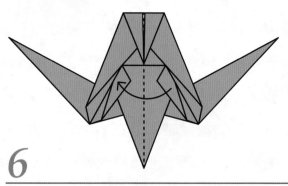

6

Valley fold in half.

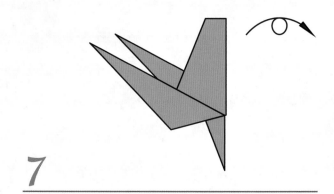

7

Rotate.

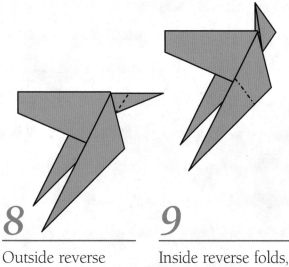

8

Outside reverse
fold.

9

Inside reverse folds,
both sides.

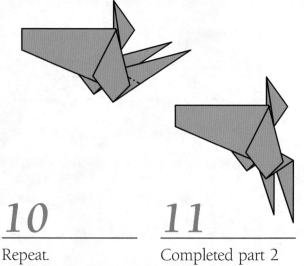

10

Repeat.

11

Completed part 2
(rear) of gazelle.

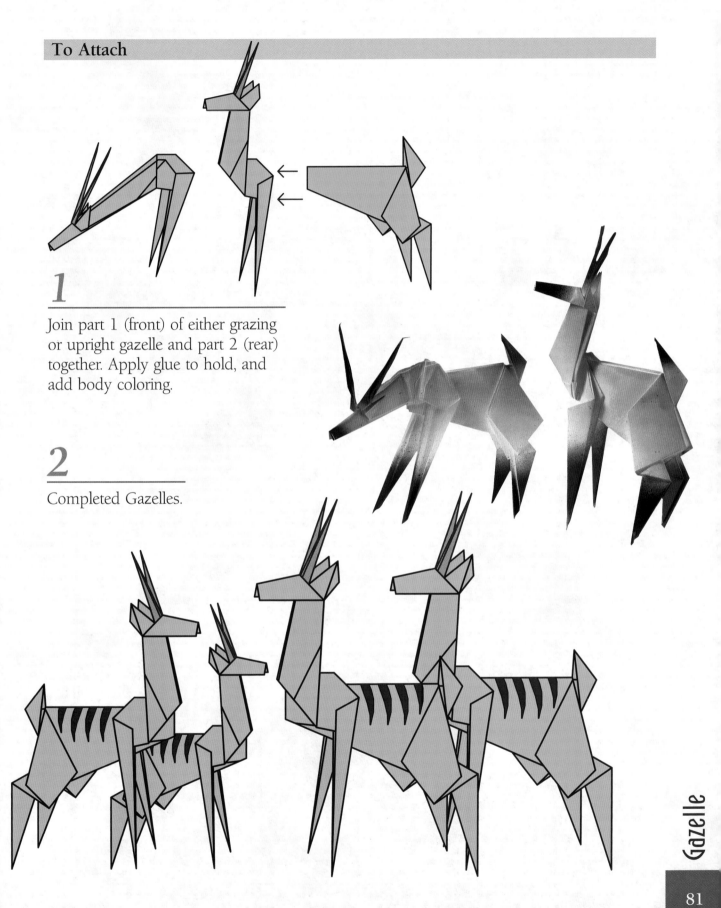

1

Join part 1 (front) of either grazing or upright gazelle and part 2 (rear) together. Apply glue to hold, and add body coloring.

2

Completed Gazelles.

Gazelle

Ostrich

(upright version)

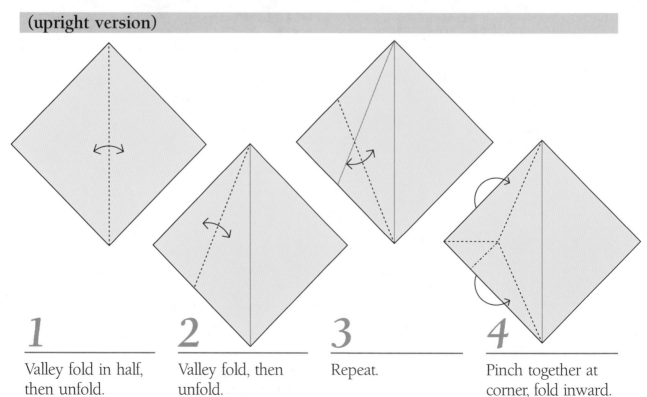

1
Valley fold in half, then unfold.

2
Valley fold, then unfold.

3
Repeat.

4
Pinch together at corner, fold inward.

82

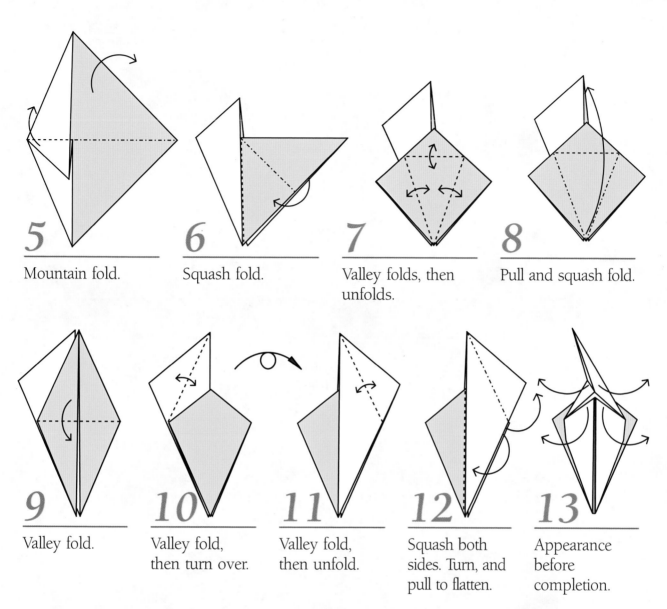

5
Mountain fold.

6
Squash fold.

7
Valley folds, then unfolds.

8
Pull and squash fold.

9
Valley fold.

10
Valley fold, then turn over.

11
Valley fold, then unfold.

12
Squash both sides. Turn, and pull to flatten.

13
Appearance before completion.

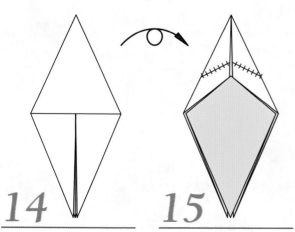

14
Turn over.

15
Cuts to front layer.

16
Valley folds.

17
Rotate vertically.

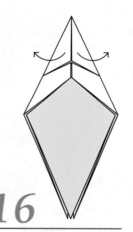

Ostrich

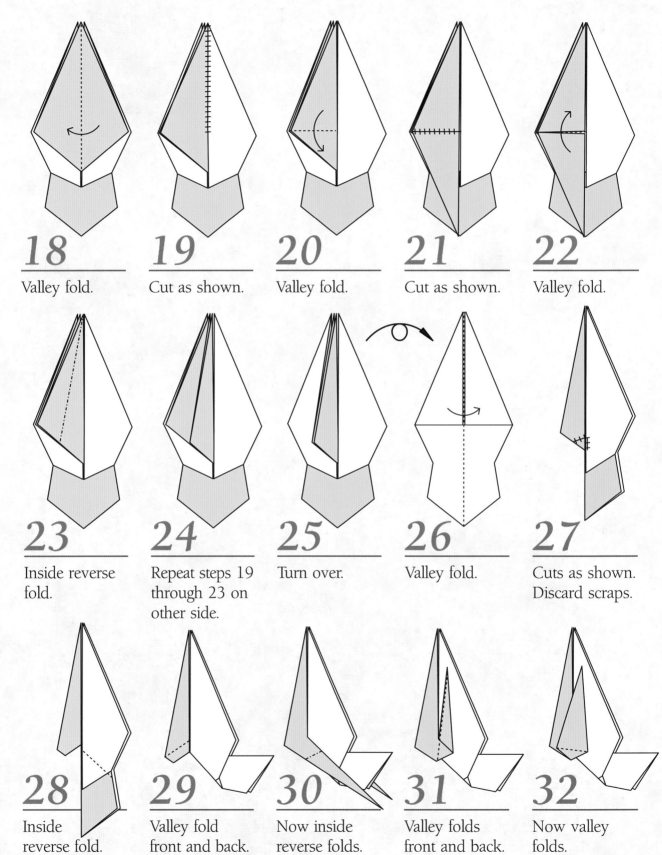

18

Valley fold.

19

Cut as shown.

20

Valley fold.

21

Cut as shown.

22

Valley fold.

23

Inside reverse
fold.

24

Repeat steps 19
through 23 on
other side.

25

Turn over.

26

Valley fold.

27

Cuts as shown.
Discard scraps.

28

Inside
reverse fold.

29

Valley fold
front and back.

30

Now inside
reverse folds.

31

Valley folds
front and back.

32

Now valley
folds.

Ostrich

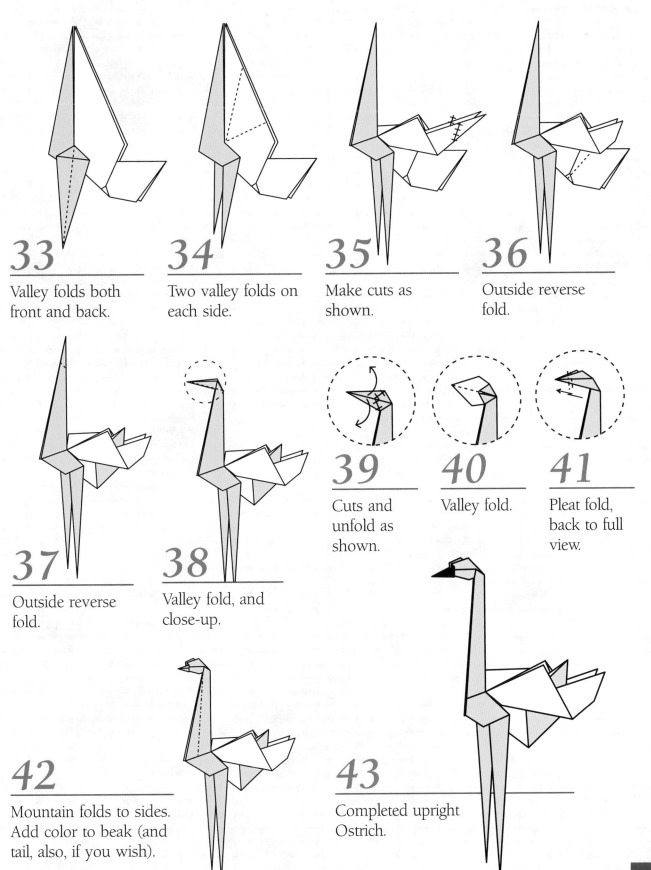

33
Valley folds both front and back.

34
Two valley folds on each side.

35
Make cuts as shown.

36
Outside reverse fold.

37
Outside reverse fold.

38
Valley fold, and close-up.

39
Cuts and unfold as shown.

40
Valley fold.

41
Pleat fold, back to full view.

42
Mountain folds to sides. Add color to beak (and tail, also, if you wish).

43
Completed upright Ostrich.

Ostrich

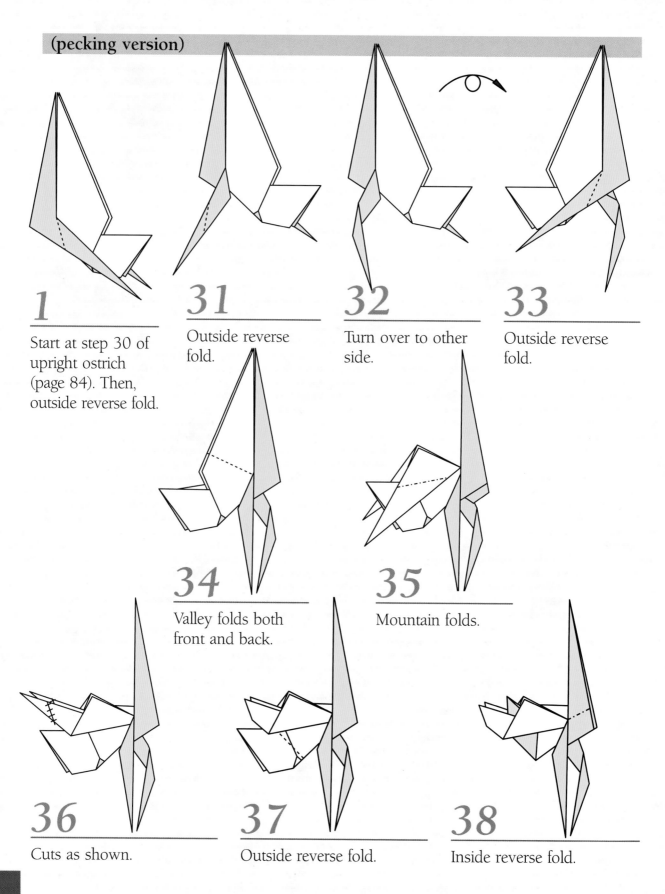

1

Start at step 30 of upright ostrich (page 84). Then, outside reverse fold.

31

Outside reverse fold.

32

Turn over to other side.

33

Outside reverse fold.

34

Valley folds both front and back.

35

Mountain folds.

36

Cuts as shown.

37

Outside reverse fold.

38

Inside reverse fold.

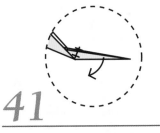

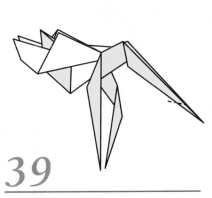

39

Inside reverse fold.

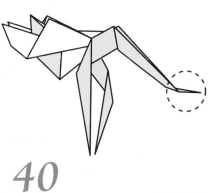

40

See close-ups for detail.

41

Cuts and valley folds.

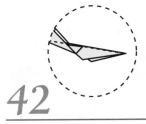

42

Valley fold.

43

Pleat fold, and back to full view.

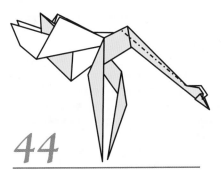

44

Mountain fold neck, then add coloring to beak (to tail also, if you wish, and bend neck to shape).

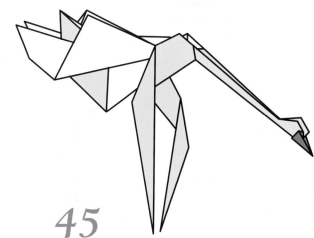

45

Completed pecking Ostrich.

Elephant

Part 1

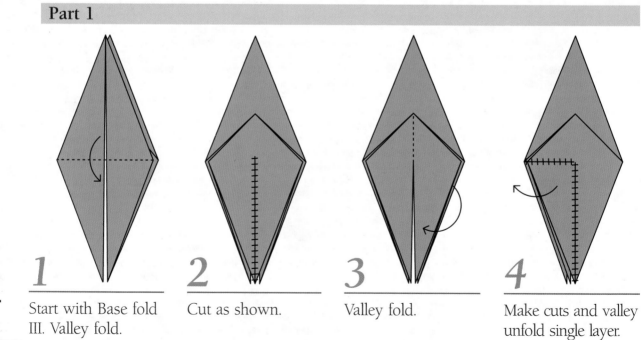

1
Start with Base fold
III. Valley fold.

2
Cut as shown.

3
Valley fold.

4
Make cuts and valley
unfold single layer.

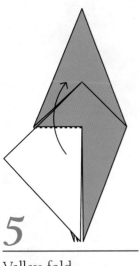

5

Valley fold.

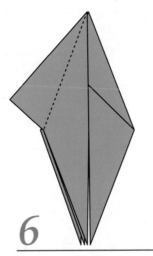

6

Valley fold.

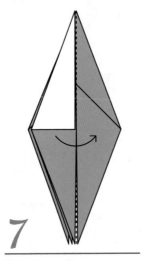

7

Valley fold.

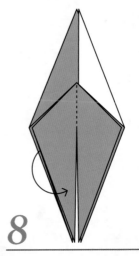

8

Valley fold.

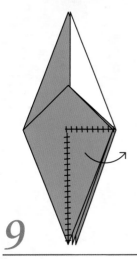

9

Cuts and valley
unfold.

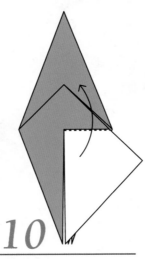

10

Valley fold.

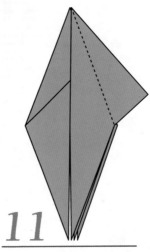

11

Valley fold.

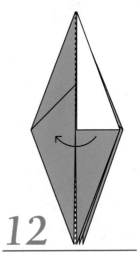

12

Valley fold.

13

Mountain fold in half.

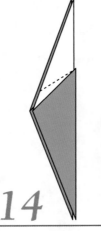

14

Valley fold front
and back.

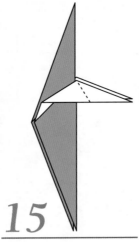

15

Repeat.

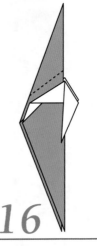

16

Outside reverse
fold.

Elephant

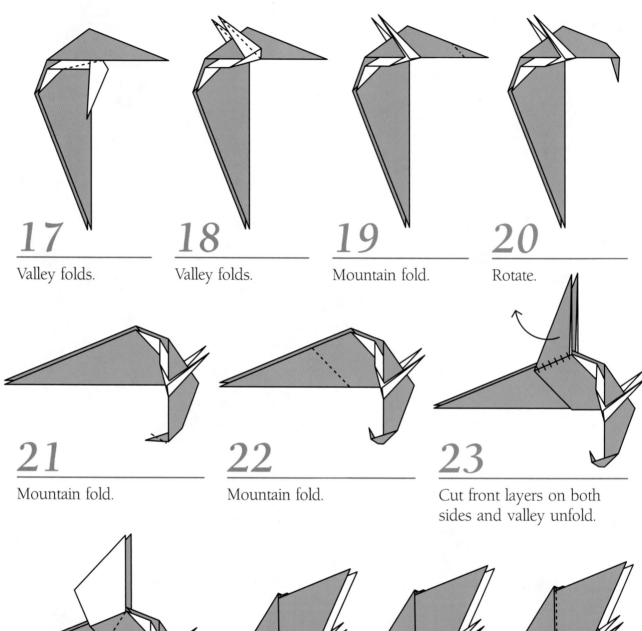

17

Valley folds.

18

Valley folds.

19

Mountain fold.

20

Rotate.

21

Mountain fold.

22

Mountain fold.

23

Cut front layers on both sides and valley unfold.

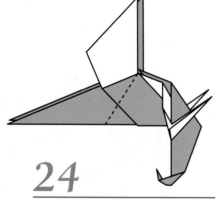

24

Valley fold both sides.

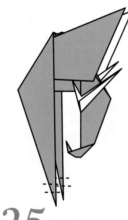

25

Double outside reverse folds.

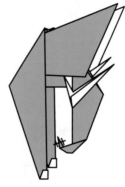

26

Cut tip as shown.

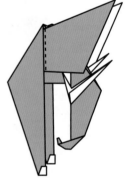

27

Valley fold both sides.

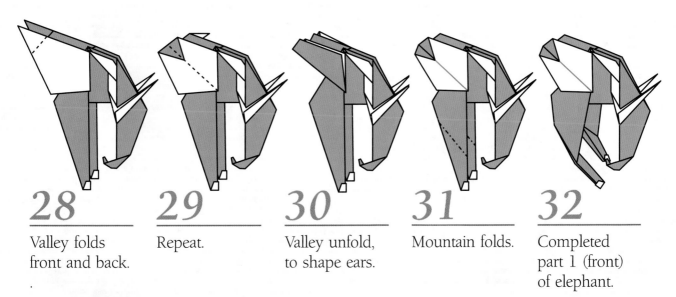

28
Valley folds
front and back.
.

29
Repeat.

30
Valley unfold,
to shape ears.

31
Mountain folds.

32
Completed
part 1 (front)
of elephant.

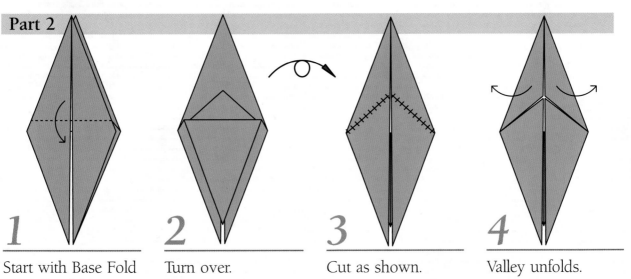

Part 2

1
Start with Base Fold
III. Valley fold.

2
Turn over.

3
Cut as shown.

4
Valley unfolds.

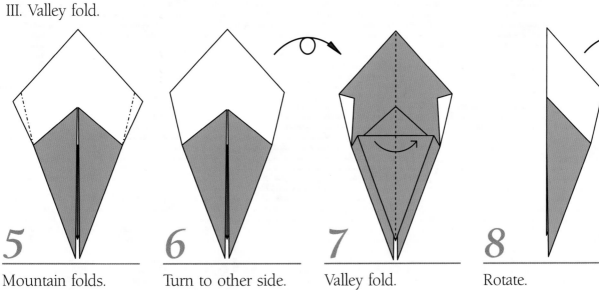

5
Mountain folds.

6
Turn to other side.

7
Valley fold.

8
Rotate.

Elephant

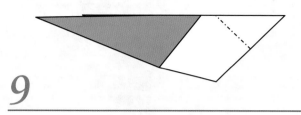

9

Inside reverse fold.

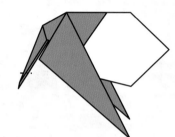

10

Valley fold both front and back.

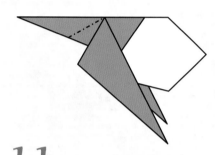

11

Inside reverse fold.

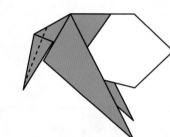

12

Valley fold both sides.

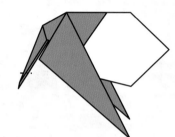

13

Inside reverse fold.

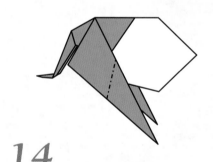

14

Inside reverse folds.

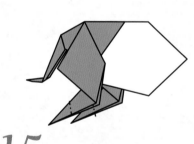

15

Inside reverse folds.

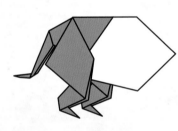

16

Rotate.

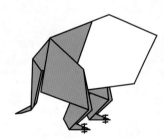

17

Cut as shown.

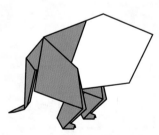

18

Completed part 2 (rear) of elephant.

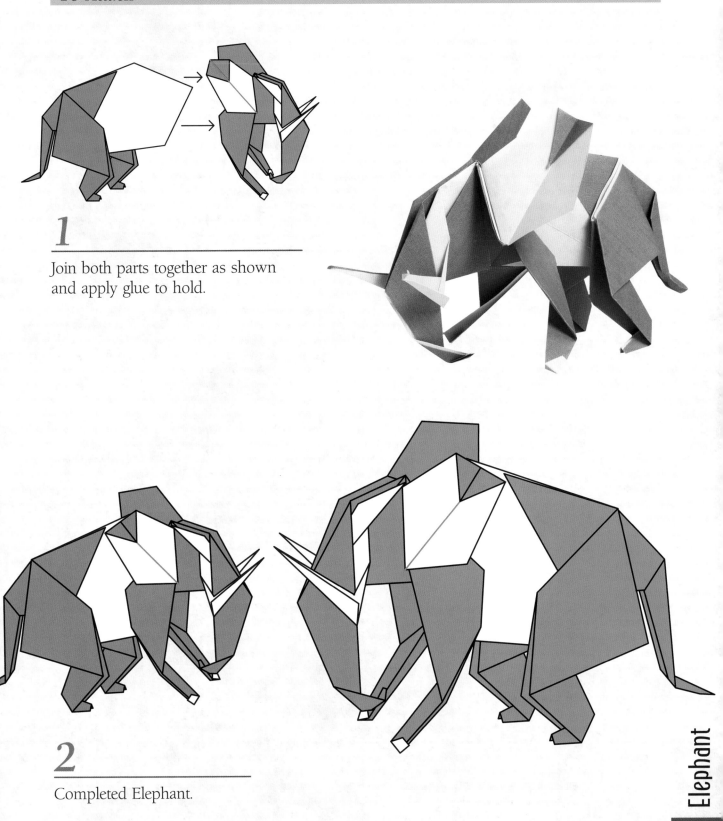

1

Join both parts together as shown
and apply glue to hold.

2

Completed Elephant.

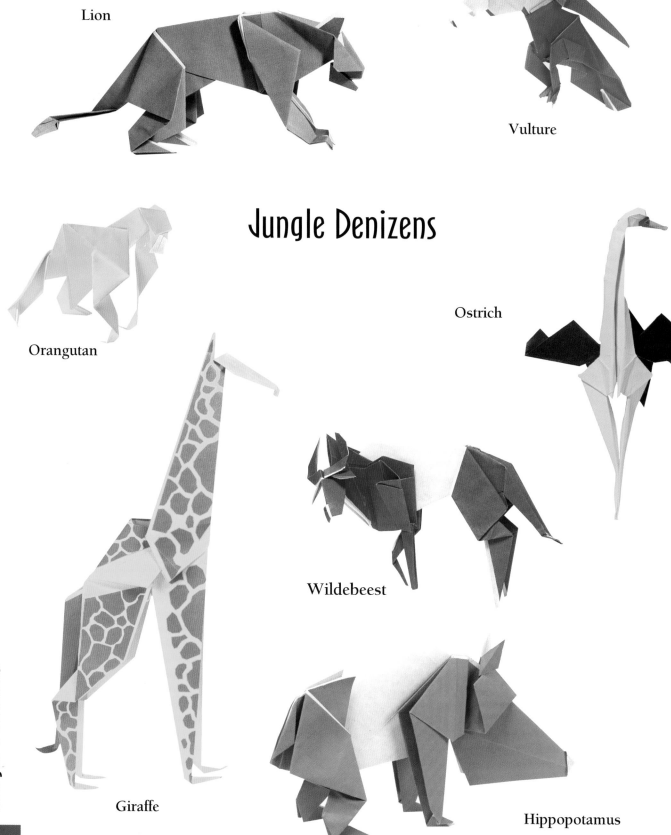

Lion

Vulture

Jungle Denizens

Orangutan

Ostrich

Giraffe

Wildebeest

Hippopotamus

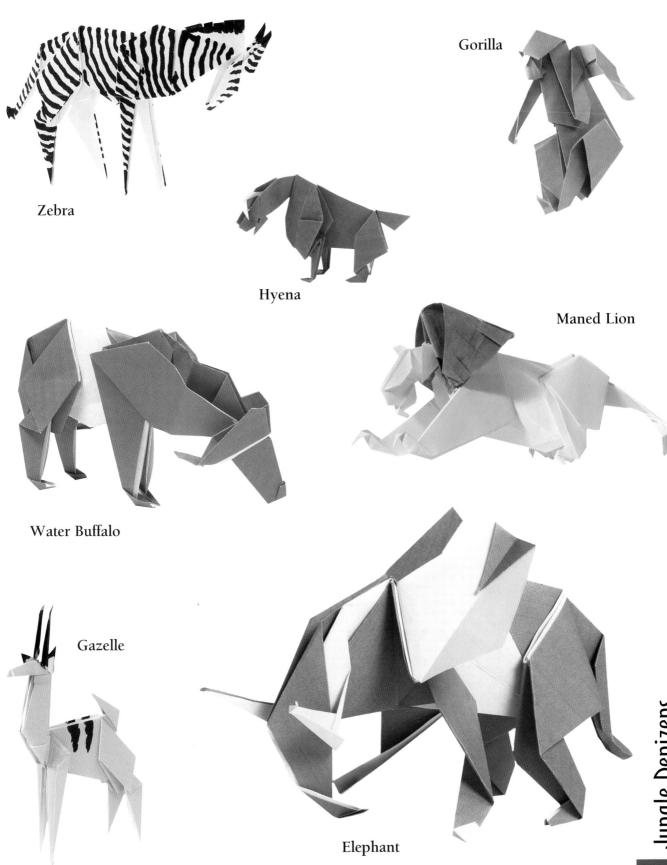

Zebra

Gorilla

Hyena

Maned Lion

Water Buffalo

Gazelle

Elephant

Index

construction lines, 4
Elephant, 88–93
finishing, 4–5
folds, base, 10–15
   I, 10
   II, 11
   III, 12–13
   IV, 14–15
folds, basic, 6–9
   inside crimp fold, 9
   inside reverse fold, 7
   kite fold, 6
   mountain fold, 6
   outside crimp fold, 9
   outside reverse fold, 7
   pleat fold, 8
   pleat fold reverse, 8

   squash fold I, 8
   squash fold II, 9
   valley fold, 6
Gazelle, 76–81
Giraffe, 32–35
Gorilla, 36–41
grazing gazelle, 78–81
Hippopotamus, 26–31
Hyena, 22–25
inside crimp fold, 9
inside reverse fold, 7
instructions, basic, 4–5
kite fold, 6
lines indication, 5
Lion, 42–47
Lion, Maned. 48–53
mountain fold, 6

Orangutan, 66–69
Ostrich, 82–87
outside crimp fold, 9
outside reverse fold, 7
paper, origami, 4
paints, 4–5
pecking ostrich, 86–87
pleat fold reverse, 8
pleat fold, 8
squash fold I, 8
squash fold II, 9
symbols/lines, 5
valley fold, 6
Vulture, 16–21
Water Buffalo, 54–59
Wildebeest, 60–65
Zebra, 70–75

Index